The War Has Ended
but the
Memory Lingers On

Christiaan Gutteling
Helen Gutteling Munday

Printed in the United States of America

Contents

"The brave, the bold, and the screwball."

PART 1—DEN HELDER

"If you can keep your head when everyone is losing his (Rudyard Kipling), then you may not understand the problem. (Christiaan Gutteling).

Egographic Record

The public record: In World War II, Christiaan Gutteling served in the Royal Netherlands Navy. They were in alliance with the United States of America and the Royal British Navies. He was a naval aviator who reached the rank of senior lieutenant navigator. He was awarded the *Bronze Cross (equivalent to the Silver Cross)* for bravery and the *Home Commemoration* Cross with a bar for the *Air War* 1940-1945.

Personal record: I am a Dutchman, for the simple reason that my parents were citizens of the Kingdom of The Netherlands. What follows is written from an egocentric point of view. It reflects not only what I perceive, understand and remember, but also reflects other people's reactions, or lack of it, to my person by word of mouth, reportage, hearsay, and body language. This is all I can give, as I have never been important, significant or famous enough to have a biographer following my every move.

I am eighty-four years of age as I write this memoir, Anno Domini 2004. My year of birth was 1920. I have forgotten many things and details which happened to me and around me sixty years ago. To help my story go with the flow and to bridge some of the gaps due to memory lapses, I invented certain trivial details which neither add nor diminish from history's broad tapestry.

I have tried hard to articulate my story and position for my invisible audience, especially for those, who cannot remotely comprehend what it is like to live under an oppressive army of German occupation in a war of attrition where no holds were barred.

The difference between understanding and not understanding is also the difference between going through an experience and trying to visualize it or imagine it. Maybe, the difference is between respect and admiration or the reverse, hate and fear.

The publishing industry has flooded the market with printed matter on World War II subjects and in particular, in The Netherlands. They described what the Engelandvaarders were up to. Engelandvaarders is the official title of those who, in wartime, crossed the North Sea or went overland via Spain, Sweden, and other routes to reach England for reasons best known to themselves. "Why do I write this report so long after the facts?" I do so at the request of some members of my family and friends.

The Dutch know this type of writing as an *ego document* wherein one uses the personal pronoun *I.* This makes the writing much easier to read without giving my feelings and opinions too much color. Read it judiciously with the knowledge that a young man in the period of 1940 to 1945 was faced with the reality of a war, enemy occupation and that going into hiding was a last resort. My story is based on actual incidents and persons. The characters are not related to any person in real life except for persons mentioned in reports and identified as such.

Note: Translations from a foreign language into Dutch or English have been placed in between brackets.

Preface

Famous writers can afford anachronism. But ordinary writers, such as me, should not take liberties with the past. If I do that and sacrifice authenticity and or if my story is not exact, I trust the reader will grant me a certain amount of license. The conditions of war and the passage of time make the tracing of historical facts all but impossible as most witnesses have died by natural or calamitous causes. Archives of The Netherlands forces were destroyed just before capitulation on May 14, 1940, on the orders of Commander-in-Chief of all sea, land and Air Forces, General H.G. Winkelman. Only a few reports of minor importance escaped destruction. The history from the *Five Day War* in the Netherlands was thus rewritten nearly entirely from the memory of those who were involved. This was quite a task for me and other historians to complete and includes the inherent flaws this sort of work entails.

The German 18th Army, under General Von Kuchler, attacked the Netherlands at approximately 03:00 hours on May 10, 1940. The Netherlands government immediately sent a coded message to the British government, stating: "The Netherlands has become Allied territory."

The Netherlands government had already mobilized approximately three hundred thousand men, while the German Eighteenth Army consisted of three divisions totaling approximately forty-five thousand men. The German first Cavalry Division attacked the Northern Province, Groningen. Their object was to advance through the province of Friesland, then cross the Zuiderzee dike and capture the naval base of Den Helder.

The German army was well equipped for that time. They had state-of-the-art military machines and used the most up-to-date *blitzkrieg* methods. The Luftwaffe Air force was used as a battlefield force. Stuka dive bombers were mobile artillery and fighters kept Allied aircraft away. Their soldiers were exceedingly well trained. Our soldiers, mostly reservists, were no match. The

4

skill of the German army was such that not even heroism and dedication could overcome them.

To appreciate this narrative in its historical context, the reader is requested to consider certain facts. The Netherlands was unsuitable for rural or urban guerrilla resistance as the flat terrain offered little scope for concealment or escape. Most resistance work was in the art of sabotage in all its forms where secrecy, stealth and individual cunning were required.

Realize also that there never was a policy or strategy for an organized resistance movement with prepared dumps of sabotage-equipment stores by either the Netherlands or the British intelligence services. Most underground resistance activities started spontaneously by single persons or small groups in isolation. They were untrained and not fully conscious of the tremendous risks involved or the fatal consequences their actions could have on them, their family, or their neighbors. Furthermore, the strategic value of a conquered and occupied Netherlands and Belgium was as a source of food and skilled forced labor for Germany. The land provided some airfields from which the Luftwaffe attacked Britain. Otherwise, the Low Countries were marginal to the overall war picture.

Last, but not least, the Germans were highly specialized and skilled in managing Controls such as; road or rail controls, identity controls, movement controls, and so on, The Germans did little about road controls in the beginning of their occupation. They only attended to certain strategic bridges and coastal prohibited areas into which no one could go, or was supposed to go, without a permit. However, as the war progressed nearly all-civilian movement was restrained.

A point of interest is that the police system in the Netherlands was comparatively simple, with only two services: the town Politie and the border and country constabulary the Marechaussee. The German's imposed a police system over the local ones. This was the Netherlands Geheime Feldpolizei (GFP). It was a secret countryside constabulary with military police, the Abwehr with their large brass breastplates over field grey uniforms and the most feared, the Sicherheitsdienst (SD) of the SS. (Shutzstaffel is a German word. Shutz means security, a man who protects you. The Shutztaffel was a highly trained technical army unit originally formed to protect Hitler.) They in turn were interpenetrated with the Geheime Staatspolizei or Gestapo. From 1942 on, the GFP and the Abwehr were under the control of the SD.

The foregoing is part of the backdrop that permeated and was part of everyday life in the German occupied countries. However, one thing that must be stated clearly is that, during the mobilization and the actual fighting, rumors flew around like confetti. No one was prepared to admit that they were utterly outwitted and outgunned by the Germans. Rumors were rampant in the Netherlands. The Dutch were nervous; rumors among them blamed a fifth column of secret Nazi supporters. Stories of lights in windows, arrows in fields, parachutists dressed as priests and nuns, and other incidents spread through the Low Countries. One particular story was that poisoned chocolates were handed out by strangers. This was practically all myth, as we now know from German and British intelligence sources. It was all nonsense.

This does show how high strung and nervous the population as they accepted these rumors with great alacrity.

Careless Talk Cost Lives was a warning sign during World War II; it was not an exaggeration or an overstatement. Those were dangerous dark times when the world was in the grip of total war. People were in constant danger of enemy agents who acted tirelessly for the country of their allegiance. Anything and anyone heard or noticed that was hostile or of importance to the war effort was transmitted to their base.

The enemy used careless talk, spoken in innocence by family, friends, colleagues or lovers, such as pillow talk, or any form of frivolous talk that had the slightest bearing on the war industry.

Railway stations names were removed, or the names were painted over. There was total blackout at night. This included all forms of lighting that may be seen by the enemy, including coastal lights from lighthouses, buoys, harbor entrance lights, and lights on any form of transport. When we as sailors or airmen approached the American or Canadian coast at night during the war, the distant glow of all that coastal lighting was like approaching a fairy-tale world.

Faith in the Future

In retrospect, one does not have to be a genius to be right. Therefore, it's safe to say that, my father, Willem Marinus Gutteling (Willem, 1878–1965), in 1936, knew what to do with me, his naughty sixteen-year-old son, Christiaan. My nickname or sobriquet was *Tip;* the eldest twin. My twin brother, Marinus (Maarten or Martin depending on your native language), was certainly not identical. He was younger by a fraction of half an hour. He was taller, more studious, more sportsmanlike, and generally better behaved. My father and mother, Henriette Christina Gutteling van Stockum (Jet, 1884–1966), must have had long discussions of what to do with their wild boy *Tip*, who was troublesome in the Primary School (De Bavinck School met den Bijbel) and in the Secondary Educational School (M.U.L.O.).

My ambition was to be a sea captain or airway pilot. As a youngster, I pleaded for it. Then, a newspaper advertisement suggested a future career in navigation with the Navy after a two-year training course in a Naval College at Den Helder Hogere Zeevaartschool, Den Helder.

After we made enquiries we were visited by Mr. Jan Middendorp, the Managing Director of that Navigational College in Den Helder. He was also a commander in the Royal Naval Reserve (KMR) who ran a *tight ship* and was known as a disciplinarian. He was tall, stood upright, broad shouldered, and always wore a bowler hat. His stern face could change quickly into a kind or amused smile and his mannerisms showed strength of purpose and command.

Mr. Middendorp convinced my parents that his Naval College was the answer to their problems, but for one easily overcome drawback. I needed a one-year Preparatory Training as my academic merits were not good enough to enter for higher navigational learning. There and then I entered into an amphibian future that would start in early January 1937. I was told of this fact and introduced to Mr. Middendorp. He was a big man with a big smiling and friendly face who said all the right things. He promised to pick me up for Den Helder when the time came to attend my Preparatory Course. I was surprised, but pleased, that I was accepted in the Preparatory Course. I took some time to absorb the notion that I was accepted in the Preparatory Course. My time had come.

I was sixteen when the time came for me to go in early January 1937. I was picked up by Mr. Middendorp to go by car from The Hague (Den Haag) to Den Helder.

I said goodbye to my parents, my siblings and my home; in short, goodbye to Beeklaan 450, our address in The Hague which became a permanent identification in my mind. Even now after sixty-seven years, I remember the telephone number but there is no one to answer it; this is so silly!

From that time on, I only returned to my family for my holidays. At the time I had no inkling of how much I would miss them in my lonely hours.

Mr. Middendorp was very kind. He had spent Christmas and New-Years in The Hague and was thus able to give me a lift.

The journey was quick and uneventful through typical flat North Holland landscapes via Leiden and Gouda and then to Den Helder. We arrived in the De Nieuwe Diep harbor area on a street named Ankerpark.

The Navigational College, (Hogere Zeevaartschool Den Helder), was an imposing three-story building at Ankerpark No.27. My students' residence was directly opposite. I was introduced to my House Master and his wife, Mr. and Mrs. de Klerk, after which Mr. Middendorp quietly disappeared to become The Director for the next three years.

This was my alma mater, my foster mother for the period of my studies. My students' residence was a one down-one upper. The living quarters for Mr. and Mrs. de Klerk were on the ground floor which was out of bounds for us. Our dining room and kitchen was upstairs along with three bedrooms for twelve boarders and our ablution section.

All our school activities and homework had to be done in the main school building and all the outside practical seamanship work was done at other harbor areas. Our bedrooms were small rooms with two bunk beds and two clothes lockers at each bunk end. Because I was the tallest student in my room, I was allocated a top bunk. Being one of the first to arrive I got to choose the North or South upper bunk; I chose the South one. That was my patch for the next three years. We were allowed to bring the minimum necessities in underwear, strong woolen jerseys, socks, scarf and gloves, warm pajamas and good rainwear. For outside work the school provided garments such as an overall, oilskin coat, and southwester. I was not allowed to wear a uniform and cap until I passed Prep year and the entrance examination to the Navigational College. My peers regarded me as a nonentity as I was not a high school graduate. To enter Navigational College, one had to have graduated from high school. All others were qualified to start Navigational College as they were high school graduates. Therefore, I was off into the great unknown with no idea of what was in store for me.

The next three days saw our two students' residences filling up with new students. I had some time to have a look around the harbor area and the town, which gave me some idea of the kind of world I had entered. Older students and officers from the Merchant Navy, who had come back for their higher grade exams to become Third, Second, First officer, or to get their Master's (Captain's) Certificate, all went to boarding houses in town.

Our daily routine started at 06:00 hours, breakfast at 07:00 hours and the school started at 08:00 hours until 12:00 hours, a cooked lunch at 12:30 hours and then school started again at 13:00 hours until 17:00 hours, and then a simple evening meal at 18:00 hours.

I must cut a long story short, for this is not an account of my years of training, but it serves as a short introductory digest to my war experiences; to wit, I passed my three years with flying colors, mainly because I quickly adapted myself to this kind of life.

I liked the subjects of the school curriculum, it applied to the practical side of seamanship, although rough and hard work in all sorts of weather conditions, loved the mathematical side of navigational problems with its spherical geometry and trig-onometry; liked working with the sextant and the practical side of sailing, was interested in the application of material handling and in the art of safe stowing; but found the international sea laws and protocol, languages, and geography tedious; but then, cartography and cosmology were most interesting. All-in-all, I did very well with high marks; a pleasant surprise to my parents.

I got to know many people in Den Helder and even had a girlfriend, Annie Smit, whom I took to the college parties, which were held twice a year. Annie, who was my age, introduced me to her parents at my first college party. She had auburn hair to her shoulders, was tall and slender with a ready smile. She designed dresses and sewed for her customers at her parents' house, where she lives. Her father was a busy small building contractor. He was tall and strong with a ruddy lined face. Annie's mother was a wonderful cook and made lovely pancakes.

Their home became my home away from home in my spare time; as so many kind citizens were doing for away from home youngsters.

What about Den Helder itself? You can become lyrical about a place, but unless you were born and bred in Den Helder, it took some time to get used to. The town had little or no character. It was drab and plain. To quote statistical data, at that time, Den Helder had approximately nine thousand nine hundred and twenty dwellings with some seventy-eight thousand citizens. Sixteen hundred persons worked at the Royal Naval Dockyard and two hundred fishermen operated a fishing fleet of forty vessels and twenty flat-bottom boats. In the harbor area along the Nieuwe Diep was The Royal Naval Establishment with a large and well-equipped naval dockyard.

Here also, was The Royal Institute for the Navy, which trained Royal Naval Officers. In addition, there was a Navigational

College, Hogere Zeevaartschool. They prepared students to become officers in the merchant navy or the civil airways. Den Helder was a twin or binary settlement; there were citizenry and there were navy; two very different concepts.

Den Helder citizens had basic universal ideals and wished for a fixed steady income, his own house, (either rented or owned), and a funeral at the local cemetery. These ideals governed the citizen's lives. The naval man wanted more out of life. He had the urge to leave this plain and drab place, to see the world and to better himself. Both groups understood each other, and in general terms, there were no rich or no poor. This near equality engendered a peaceful coexistence at the end of a single railway track at North Holland's lands end.

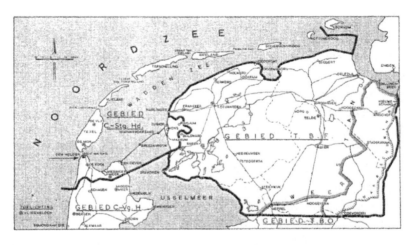

Kaart nr 1   Overzicht van de gebieden van de T.B.F. en de C.-Stg. Hd.

GEBIED/TERRITORY : - C.Stg.Hd. - Commandant van de Stelling van Den Helder.
                   - T.B.F.   - Territoriale Bevelhebber in Friesland,
                                   Groningen en Drente.
                   - Vg.H.   - Vesting Holland.

The sea and the storms made and created this lands end and had formed the character of its inhabitants. A great many of them had walked the tide line along the sandy beach or on the dikes or along the extreme end of the harbor where the sea flowed over the blue-black basalt blocks which were the actual lands end. They listened to the voice of the wind and the sea which was part of their universe.

Line of Defense

The Netherlands consists of eleven Provinces of which two are called Holland, i.e. North-Holland and South-Holland. Both face west; facing the North Sea and England. Den Helder is situated at the top of North-Holland, roughly forty degrees forty-five minutes east of the meridian of Greenwich and fifty degrees to fifty-two minutes north of the equator. It is roughly at the same height as Nottingham in the United Kingdom. In olden times, the naval and merchant fleets found a safe berth on the roadstead of the island of Texel and to the east of the small town of Den Helder. In the years 1780 to 1784; which the Dutch call the Fourth English War, they deepened and enlarged a coastal creek which became the excellent harbor, the Nieuwe Diep. In 1781 it became, and still is, the official Naval Port. Napoleon visited Den Helder in 1811 to order the enlargement and strengthening of the coastal defenses at the top of the Province of North Holland and the southern part of the island of Texel. This also included the Naval Port Nieuwe Diep and all around Den Helder in defense of the English.

This work was completed in 1813 but was constantly added to throughout the 19th century and became known as the Stelling van Den Helder. Stelling translates as Point or Strong Point. It is a Line of Defense stretching across all the Friesian Islands (Wadden Eilanden) to the German border.

This military activity surrounded the small town of Den Helder, where some of the burghers found useful employment.

Just before 1940, the Stelling of Den Helder consisted of the following territories: the top of North-Holland, including the Naval Harbor, its wharves, warehouses and shipyards, its Naval College and its coastal defenses; all the Friesian Islands (Wadden Eilanden) to the German border; and the dike across the Zuider Zee. This was known as the Afsluitdijk with its fortifications in Friesland (Wonstelling, North Holland) at Den Oever. In other words, the whole top of The Netherlands was under the command of a Rear

Admiral commanding all the necessary sea, land, and air forces in his area.

For all this military activity, the civilian population of Den Helder remained small as nearly all members of the forces came from elsewhere. The established grades for battle readiness were normal (normaal); increased (verhoogd); and complete (volledig). The last two grades demanded a great degree of endurance and stamina from the armed forces when battle stations were manned and in a state of readiness. This was exhausting and could not be maintained indefinitely. The antiaircraft artillery had to be ready for near instant reaction to fire and be fully prepared with ample ammunition at hand for a sustained attack.

Increased and complete readiness were therefore used only in extreme necessity and then only for as short a duration as possible. In battle conditions this stretched for as long as required with, hopefully, relief troops standing by.

A period of great tension and uneasiness developed on April 9, 1940, when German forces invaded Denmark and Norway. By the end of April, the tension abated somewhat. However, on May 7, 1940, the commander in chief of all our forces instructed us to be extremely alert. He stopped all leaves and recalled all who were on leave; to tighten and increase all guard duties and so on.

On May 9 at 20:45 hours, the increased preparedness order was given to all airfields, antiaircraft artillery, air forces and the Civil Defense to be ready in defense of airborne and parachute attacks, with the message: "Intelligence from our borders give alarming reports; be very much on your guard."

At 23:15 hours, an order was given to all forces for complete preparedness to commence at 03:00 hours May 10, 1940.

The commander of the-Stelling Den Helder followed this up immediately with the order to all units of the fleet, army and air forces under his command to be completely prepared. This meant: laying mines between the islands, closing harbors, stationing of minesweepers in case mines were dropped by air; switching off all fleet lights and coastal and harbor lights, a total blackout of towns and villages and others. It included manning all bunkers and strong points, preparedness of the coastal artillery, and blocking all roads and open places that could be used to land aircraft or gliders. (Old and wrecked cars and similar scrap had been collected and bought from dumps and car wrecking firms for this purpose. They had been distributed and lay ready for blocking purposes at preselected positions.) In addition, anything else that could effectively deter the attacks was used.

This was "It." All those concerned waited for the inevitable; or as the Americans would say, "Hunkered down for action." It was quite an eerie experience for our forces.

The sea was never bluer in the Marsdiep, the seagulls more white, the cloud banks more majestic, or the fragrance of the roses and lilacs more sweet than in the early days of May 1940. Den Helder was at peace and there was a general feeling of tranquility within the citizenry. They thought that with our army and navy and our overseas friends, we were well protected. And, of course, the Netherlands was neutral. This went against all better knowledge and judgment. The latest news reports flooding in should have been worrying, but somehow, they did not seem to be of much concern to the man-on-the-street.

Those days were cheerful with music. The Royal Naval band gave musical evenings under smoky torchlight that made the brass instruments glitter and shine. Every evening saw the cafes and restaurants packed full with soldiers and sailors and their friends; the Spoorstraat, a favorite shopping street, was filled with strolling people and the Casino was filled with the youthful dancing the night away. Den Helder was carefree!

The evening of May 9 was sultry with a red sundown and with nothing of importance happening. The night was still with the fragrance of white and purple lilacs wafting around and it seemed as if their world was holding its breath! What for? For the start of a war that no one had believed could happen to them.

In the early hours of May 10, the war started followed by five days that felt as if it was one long endless day.

Addendum: The military information was given to me by the Hoofd Bureau Documentatie En Informatie Van De Instituut Voor Militaire Geschiedenis (Head office for Documentation and Information Of The Institute For Military History) in The Hague.

Finals

May 10, 1940

Three years have passed. I am twenty years old and a senior student studying hard for my final examinations for the AS Certificate (Aspirant Stuurman or Fourth Officer of the Merchant Navy. This senior school year was a real slog; I had worked very hard. My previous college years were very good. I received high marks which pleased my parents.

I must have fallen asleep over my books, when someone was shouting something that, at first, I did not fully comprehend. It slowly penetrated, "Wake up, wake up and listen—planes, low flying and lots of them." This was strange as it was just before three in the morning and stranger still when we heard the staccato sound of antiaircraft artillery opening up not far from us in the harbor area. Through our windows the other students and I observed the night sky filling up with tracers going up all over. Wow! It was like beautiful fireworks! But what was this all about? Maneuvers by our fleet and air force or what? All of a sudden, the racket stopped followed by an eerie silence. North of us over the island of Texel, we could see tracers going up without sound because of the distance. Then that also stopped.

By now, our whole college residence was up and about and in a state of agitation. Everyone was talking at the same time until our housemaster blew his whistle. He told us to, "Pipe down and listen up." "For the last fortnight you have been busy and studying hard preparing for your finals. You had little or no time, for anything else but studying and attending the extra preparatory lessons. Therefore, you are not well informed about happenings outside. Now the bubble has burst. Our country has been under threat from Germany for some time. It seems that this morning, we were attacked by German forces. I surmise that those planes we heard were laying mines in our waters and waterways to prevent our fleet from moving out. I will keep you informed as soon as I know more, but for now, calm down, it is already getting light. Get dressed and come down for early breakfast. Any questions?" There were no questions as everyone was speechless!

We looked at each other, quietly did what had to be done and went downstairs to breakfast. We were hungry, subdued and thinking of our families and friends. Mrs. de Klerk's breakfast consisted of steaming porridge, brown bread with butter, jam, or cheese and a glass of milk. It was a typical breakfast and we could eat as much as we liked.

Mrs. de Klerk told us her husband was at a meeting of schoolmasters and instructors to decide who would take over from Mr. Middendorp (Ome Jan or Uncle John, as we called him), our managing director. He was called up some days before as he was a commander in the Royal Naval Reserve. He would probably be away for a time and could leave with the fleet to other parts of the world. All we were told was that all final year students had to muster at 08:00 in classroom number one and await further instructions.

At 07:50 all final year students were sitting quietly in classroom number one. Promptly at 08:00 our mathematics teacher, Mr. Grobben, entered sucking heavily on his pipe, blowing clouds of smoke around him and staring at us before he said, "Gentlemen, by now you have completed nearly all the subjects for your final exam and have two written and three oral exam subjects remaining. The two written exams will be done tomorrow in this classroom, one in the morning and the other in the afternoon. For the oral exams, we require three experienced government exam board appointed sea captains, they have not yet arrived in Den Helder. We do not have the slightest idea what will happen under the present emergency conditions or even when we can contact them as all telephone lines have been seized by our armed forces. You will be further informed as soon as we know more. "You are dismissed, and I wish you success with your exams."

At the end of this first day of war, the Germans had downed nearly the whole Dutch Air Force and had full command of the air. They had crossed the Meuse and had taken the Moerdijk Bridge near Dordrecht and Rotterdam. Dutch Royal Navy ships, the cruiser Hr. Ms. Jacob van Heemskerk, one destroyer and seven submarines, of which two were new and incomplete, left for Scottish waters to fight another day. Naval key personnel such as reservists, technicians, midshipmen under training and as many valuable technical stores as could be stowed, were packed on board of these vessels to get them out of Holland and to the British Isles. Note: On that day, May 10, 1940, Winston Churchill became Prime Minister of Great Britain.

May 11, 1940

We did our two written exams which left us utterly clapped out. As tired as we were, most of us went into town in the late afternoon to visit friends and to get the latest news about the war situation. I went to the family Smit and found them in good health but very worried about the future. I had evening meal with them, prepared by Annie.

We spent the rest of the evening listening to the radio. As I had to be back in my college residence by 22:00 and as it was late, I ran for it. Not knowing that a curfew was proclaimed by the military, I ran slap bang into a roadblock trying to cross the railway line. As I was running, I counted myself lucky not to have been shot or manhandled as the armed naval chaps were trigger-happy with rumors of German parachutists about. I was in plainclothes and not in uniform, so I had to use my naval college pass to get myself off the hook and allowed to proceed with a warning to be careful. There was a notice in my boarding house to the effect that two of the sea captains had arrived and that the oral exams would start the next day. We were to check the schedule on the college notice board to find out when and where each of us was to report.

In Den Helder the second day of the war went by with the movement of troops, in and around the town, setting up road-blocks. Heavily armed sailors and marines assembled and boarded army lorries and touring coaches to be transported to the frontline at the

Wonstelling in Friesland to strengthen the defense of the Afsluitdijk, the 40 km long dike across the Zuider Zee.

Den Helder turned from a sleepy town into a hive of activity with troop movements to and from the North Eastern front line with fresh troops going, exhausted and wounded troops coming back.

For us final year students of the Naval College, we were back studying for the oral exams. All the other students were sent home, at least those who could make it home by one means or another. Those who could not stayed on at their boarding house. Families could still not be contacted by phone. At the end of the second day of the war, the Germans had broken the back of the main Dutch resistance near Wageningen by taking the Grebbelinie and Wonstelling in Friesland. The English cruiser, HMS Arethuse, and two destroyers escorted two merchant ships carrying Dutch bullion, large stocks of diamonds and other valuables back to England from the port of IJmuiden.

May 12, 1940, Whit Sunday

The early morning of Whitsuntide (het Pinksterfeest or Pentecost for the Jews) started with the arrival of the British destroyer HMS Griffin in the roadstead of Den Helder. The commander of this destroyer was under orders to find out if any assistance could be given and was told that if, fighter aircraft and bombers required a place to land terrain would be made ready in the Wieringermeer Polder, after which the destroyer would leave. This never happened, as three days later the Dutch forces had capitulated.

The oral-exam schedule, on the notice board in the main Naval College building, showed that I had two sessions today and my final one tomorrow morning. I found them quite easy. It was a relief to have nearly all the exams behind me. That night I went to sleep early to be refreshed for tomorrow's last exam.

The third day of war saw bitter fighting down south in Brabant, Dordrecht and Rotterdam, outside The Hague and in the North in Friesland. This is where the Germans tried to get hold of the Afsluitdijk across the Zuider Zee. They did not get it until after the capitulation was signed. Right to the end, the Stelling Den Helder prevented the Germans from getting into North-Holland via the Afsluitdijk, but these successes did not change the final outcome. The British destroyer HMS Codrington embarked with the Crown Princess Juliana and her family at the port of Ijmuiden and took them to England.

May 13, 1940, Whit Monday

The weather was beautiful and sunny, but a war situation that held no prospects for the Dutch, it really was grim.

TRANSLATION OF OVERLEAF DOCUMENT   (PAGE *15*)

CERTIFICATE
IN COMPLIANCE WITH CLAUSE 21 FIRST PARAGRAPH,
INDUSTRIAL-EDUCATION LAW

The Board and the Delegates for the final examinations of the Navigational Schools and the Director and Teachers of the Navigational School in Den Helder declare that *Christiaan Gutteling*, born on *8 April 1920*, in *Buitenzorg*, has successfully carried out the final exams according to the curriculum A.S., taken at the above mentioned school in *May 1940*.

For the Board and the Delegates,
the Chairman
Signed

Den Helder the *31 July 1940*

Signature of the Examinee
Signed

For the Director and Teachers,
the Director
Signed

Her Majesty Queen Wilhelmina and her personal staff, surrounded by a platoon of heavily armed Royal Marines, was brought safely to the English port of Harwich by the British destroyer HMS Hereward. Members of the Dutch government and Allied legation staff were evacuated on the destroyer HMS Windsor. All this was done in time to prevent capture by the Germans, the signing and legalization of an official capitulation and a possible peace treaty. Heavy fighting went on all over with the Germans rapidly gaining ground. They soon reached the outskirts of Rotterdam. The only Dutch success was at the Afsluitdijk in the Stelling of Den Helder, where the Germans were stopped and pushed back. It was to no avail in the overall picture of this conflict.

For me, it was a matter of doing my last oral exam in the late morning. I felt I had done reasonably well, but who knows? I was now free to go home, if that was possible in the present circumstances with troops, friendly or foe, all over the place. They were heavily armed and trigger happy and the railways and roadways were blocked by army convoys or fleeing refugees. The telephone lines were still blocked, and postal services had ceased, so I stayed in the students' residence for the time being.

Quo Vadis

As soon as the war started, I knew I was in a bind, a trap, because my future as a merchant naval officer depended on getting a job at sea as soon as I qualified from the Naval College as an Aspirant Stuurman. I received the AS Certificate, on July 31, 1940. I was now on the lowest rung on the ladder of my naval career as a Fourth Officer. To get to the next rung of Third Officer, I had to have one year, i.e. three hundred and sixty-five sea duty days of experience logged as Fourth Officer and then return to the Naval College to study and sit for the exam for Third Officer. In roughly the same manner, you could advance to Second and First Officer and eventually sit for the Captain's Certificate.

The war really put a stop to my naval career unless I could get away from the Netherlands. I worried about what to do and how to do it against the odds of a German occupation. I did not have the foggiest idea of how to get out of this bind, but somehow or other, I felt that I should go-with-the-flow and keep a low profile until I knew more about the German occupation. This meant hiding for a while until things became clear. I decided to have a talk with Mr. Smit.

Pax Germanicus

Tuesday, May 14, 1940

The German Air Force (Luftwaffe) savagely dive-bombed Rotterdam to end the heavy street fighting. This not only ended the Dutch resistance in Rotterdam, but effectively wiped out this open city leaving it burning fiercely. General Winkelman, the Commander in Chief of the Netherland forces, now had to decide whether to fight to the end or surrender. Rotterdam was wiped out and the Germans threatened to do the same to Utrecht and other towns and there was little support from our Allies. A decision to carry on would result in the slaughter of our troops and civilians. The General decided that surrender was inevitable. At about 17:00 hours, he ordered all Netherland's forces to lay down their arms and surrender to the nearest German troops. The German High Command was informed of the surrender and the official surrender ceremony between the top commanders happened that night in the North section. The surrender was to the German commander of the First Cavalry Division in Sneek, in Friesland.

The Netherlands government never officially capitulated. They had moved to London with Her Majesty Queen Wihelmina to carry on the fight for liberation from the Germans.

At about 14:00 hours, Acting Managing Director, Mr. Grobben, told us that the German troops would probably arrive the following day. He was advised to tell us that no one knew how the Germans would treat us. We could be viewed as a semi military institution sent into a concentration camp with our forces.

"My advice," he said, "is that you get out of your uniform, into civilian clothes and move away from the Naval College if you do not want to risk becoming prisoners of war. But whatever you decide, do it quickly."

He hardly finished speaking, when many of us ran to our Student Residence changed into civvies and packed a small case as we could not carry all our belongings and made a quick getaway. I went to the Smit family house: my first attempt at hiding. I had not

25

decided what I would do next and hoped to discuss matters with Mr. Smit: I hoped he could find a solution.

Their house was too small to accommodate me for very long. I hoped first to clear out of this military zone and then make a viable plan to go to my parents' house in The Hague and then, who knows?

There was no roadblock on the railway crossing on my way to the Smit family house. In fact, that part of town was eerily quiet. It was about 17:00 hours.

The family was home and seemed to be glad to see me but questioned my civvies and hand luggage. I was also carrying my winter overcoat, raincoat and was wearing a hat, in fact, I was loaded.

"Where on earth are you going?" was the question.

"Where the wind blows me." was my reply.

"I am on the run and it is a long story. I will tell you all about it if I may sit down."

They heard me out and said, "You've got troubles. Of course you can stay—we'll work out something—but for now, relax and have something to eat."

I felt like a balloon deflating with relief and relaxed. I never thought it could feel so good to relax. I felt safe.

We had our meal, then talked and talked and talked about the war and what was going to happen and about our country's surrender and what the Germans would be like. At about 20:10 hours we stopped talking and quietly listened to the drone of many large aircraft approaching from the east. We ran outside into the garden and saw many planes—why so many? Suddenly we heard the first loud whistling, followed by a very loud explosion, the ground trembled and we saw a reddish hazy, glow somewhere near the station which nearby. We were shocked by the blast and noise of it and ran inside the house.

Mr. Smit quickly regained his composure, ran into the kitchen and removed everything from below the concrete kitchen-sink including the shelves. He told us to get under the concrete slab and gave each of us a large pan or bucket to put on our heads. Primitive but reassuring! He ran into the bathroom and filled the bath with water in case the water supply was damaged; he was certainly on the ball! We sat under the concrete slab listening to the roar and shudder of bomb blasts for seventy minutes. We were shaken to the core and fearful that the bombers would return.

Mr. Smit checked his house which seemed to be in order. Then he went to the neighbors and found them to be shaken but all right. After a stiff drink, we all calmed down and went to sleep; or at least tried to sleep. I slept on a spare mattress on the lounge floor. The remainder of the night was comparatively quiet, broken from time to time, with the howling sirens of the fire brigade and ambulances.

About thirty German bombers had arrived over Den Helder at 20:15 hours on May 14,1940. With Den Helder still a strong military target and remembering what they did to Rotterdam, they intended to wipe out Den Helder and its harbor, workshop and dockyard areas. This was after the surrender and white flags had been placed at strategic points, Dutch forces did not respond but waved white flags. There was a delay in the message that the Dutch were flying white flags to the German Bombers from Germany. The Dutch did not know of the delay and were not prepared to fight back. The German bomber crews must have been surprised not to have met opposition and saw the white flags. They radioed their base, stopped the bombing and returned to Germany.

The German bomber crews under strict orders, bombed and machine gunned the area for seventy minutes after dropping thirty bombs in spite of the white flags. This resulted in the death of twenty-eight people, twenty badly wounded and some bunkers and about twenty-five housing complexes in a comparatively small town destroyed.

Wednesday, May 15, 1940

The commander of the Stelling of Den Helder, with his naval and army staff, went to the town of Sneek in the Province of Friesland during the night of May 14 where they met the German Commander of the First Cavalry Division in the Hotel Wijnberg for formal surrender discussions.

The German commander opened the meeting with two questions:

The first question: the German troops were under fire from heavy artillery they did not know of. What and where were they? The reply was: From Hr. Ms. Johan Maurits van Nassau, a ship of our navy.

The second question: We heard heavy explosions from the German forces the direction of Den Helder this evening. What were they? The reply was: a bombardment by the German Air Force after the surrender was declared and arms were laid down. The dike across the Zuider Zee never fell into German hands until this surrender ceremony. This took tough fighting by sailors and marines who were brought by buses and coaches from Den Helder to the front. The first German troops arrived in Den Helder on the 15th and on the island of Texel on the May 18, 1940. The German First Cavalry Division went back to Germany on May19 to be replaced by occupational forces and administrative staff.

Goodbye "Den Helder"

The next morning Mr. Smit and I took an early walk into town and found that many houses were destroyed and many more damaged. The water mains were badly damaged, the town smelled of smoke, dust and smoldering wood and the streets were full of broken glass and masonry. As we walked back saddened by what we had seen, a car with a loudhailer announced that the Public Health Department requested all citizens to gather at their nearest school, church or street corner as soon as possible; medical teams gave anti-cholera injections. This started a stir. We hurried home and collected Mrs. Smit and Annie and went to a school nearby. A taxi with a red cross flag arrived with a nurse from the Royal Naval Hospital and a first aid helper. They made short-work of injecting our group.

After breakfast, Mr. Smit said that he would go to my student residence to collect the rest of my belongings. On his return, he told us that an advanced party of German troops had just arrived in town, with the main body of troops close by. Mr. Smit advised that it would be safer for me to stay with them for a couple of days until the roads cleared. Then he would take me to his cousin's farm in the Wieringermeer Polder not far South of Den Helder where I could stay if I was willing to give a hand on the farm. Three days later in the early hours of the morning I said a fond farewell to Mrs. Smit. Mr. Smit, Annie and I went south on bicycles with all my belongings distributed between us. We met his cousin, Mr. Jan de Fries, at Slootdorp. He led us to his farm where we met the rest of his family. After a hearty lunch, I said goodbye to Annie and her father, which was very sad. If goodbye is a contraction of God be with you, then that was what we really meant.

Addendum

Den Helder remained a military target. Overnight, the Germans were holding it; the enemy was now the British, our Allies. Now, the German Navy and Army had to defend Den Helder. They brought in a great amount of army hardware; searchlights, all sorts of antiaircraft artillery, antitank guns, and more.

The Germans were under constant air surveillance and air attacks. It did not take long before the exodus of a citizenry scared out of their wits started. Annie Smit was one of them. Some time later, she found a haven for a while in my father's house in The Hague.

The Navigational College was closed by the German Authority in 1942. Right from the beginning of the German occupation banned all weather reports for navigational purposes, tide tables, sea and air almanacs for security reasons. They were supplied by special permission for such undertakings as sea rescue, coastal shipping and sea fishing and kept under lock-and-key to be returned after the expiration date. Navigational training facilities forbidden to operate until further notice.

In looking back at the five-year war from 1940 to 1945, Den Helder suffered 117 air attacks. Approximately 180 died, scores were wounded, and the town was severely damaged. Allied attacks aimed at the German defense works and warships in the harbor, causing collateral damage to the town. They never aimed at wiping out Den Helder but brought hardship and grief and did great damage to a small town.

Den Helder also lost twenty-eight resistance fighters. They were shot by firing squads, died in prison or concentration camp. Some of them were radio operators keeping the British intelligence service informed.

Netherlands forces made a stand against the German Army and Air Force, driven by the ferocity, weight in war equipment and new methods of assault of the Blitzkrieg and bombing. They reeled from successive waves of Junkers eighty-seven dive bombers, the dreaded Stukas, tanks, infantry and artillery, before giving up to prevent further slaughter.

The Germans maintained that The German Reich had no imperial designs on the Netherlands. As a conciliatory gesture, all POWs were released after our capitulation.

When war with Germany broke out, an indistinct telegram was transmitted to the Merchant Navy of the Netherlands. It was sent all over the world stating, "The enemy has invaded The Netherlands." Which enemy? England or Germany? The Netherlands deepest wish was always to remain neutral! Had the British preempted the Germans? Many Dutch merchant ships in or near British or British colonial harbors were not taking any chances. They bolted out of these harbors to get away from British territorial areas, such as De Christiaan Huygens, near Colombo, until a telegram clarified the situation.

PART 2—DEN HAAG

"Trust is hard to evaluate, harder to gain,
and easy to lose."

German Governance

The Netherlands was governed by three separate functionaries under German occupation; all three handpicked by Hitler. These three separate, mutually cooperating departments and their chiefs were as follows:

Civil Affairs: Dr. Artur von SeyssInquart, an Austrian, was the ReichsIkommissar, the highest occupation authority in the Netherlands.

Military Affairs: Luftwaffe General E.C. Christianse, Commander of the armed services in the Netherlands, which included the "Abwehr"; the German armed forces secret service.

SS (Schutzstaffel), the defense squad of National Socialism or Nazism: Obergruppenführer (Lieutenant General) Hans Albin Rauter, an Austrian.

The Dutch were concerned with the activities of the German secret services under control of the SS, whose power was ubiquitous and pervaded into all the affairs of the country. The Sicherheits Polizei (security police) was part of the *SD* (Sicherheitsdienst or security service), which was a subsection of the SS, better known as the notorious Gestapo (Geheime Staatspolizei), and was setup by Herman Goring, Chief of the Luftwaffe, and staffed mainly by members of the SS.

Hans Rauter, the SS boss in the Netherlands, was intelligent, hard-working and energetic, but ruthless; a devout Nazi and the archenemy of all underground, undercover and resistance activities against Hitler and the Germans. Under Rauter, were four successive Befehlshabers der Sicherheitspolizei (commanders of the security police). Dr. W. Harster was one. It was Haster who recruited his fellow Bavarian, Major Joseph Schreider and put him in charge of counterespionage and counter sabotage. Schreider had been a professional police officer, a border guard working on the Swiss frontier. Schreider was small and almost bald with a heavy round head, pasty face with a drinker's nose, which extended a flabby and well-manicured little hand from a corpulent body. He exuded joviality and warmth and was a virtual wolf in sheep's clothing.

Schreider, with a sharp, intellectual, quick thinking brain, could pick up a British trained agent by falling into conversation with him in a bar, recognizing the cigarette he was offered as one of a sort the British parachuted in, making the man tipsy, putting him up for the night at a police flat, and arresting him over breakfast.

He also taught his helpers to spot British fountain pens, knives, scissors, watches, pencils and even shoes at a glance. This was not to the credit of the British secret service, the S.O.E. (Special Operations Executive).

All British agents' clothes looked Dutch. But they were all identical; the same shade, pattern and cut. Even their briefcases looked the same. This compelled most agents to work and live well apart which diminished their effective teamwork. Many British agents carried little notebooks in which they jotted information, such as names and addresses of probable helpers.

These agents were expected to carry a great deal in their heads, such as bogus life stories, and more. But many stories were not thoroughly checked before taking off; again with fatal consequences.

The height of incompetence was falsified Dutch identity cards used to give the agents false identities. These cards were poorly made with the wrong watermark. Where the Royal Lions of the Netherlands heraldic insignia should be, they had lions facing in the same direction instead of facing each other and they looked more like kangaroos than lions. London's incompetence was disastrous. All it did was get their agents and Dutch helpers killed. It was not a gentleman's game. It was not a glorified escapade of friendly, decent people. Expecting the Germans to be likewise was deadly.

These young, eager agents were not well schooled in hardnosed, tough underground activities, nor did they know much of the day to day living conditions. They were given coins. When they arrived, they found the Germans had removed Dutch coinage and replaced it with a new set. They were lucky that many Dutch people did not report them. British staff officers' incompetence and plain local treachery threw away too many lives.

Patriotism and heroism were not enough when an agent was captured as the agent was in a weak position at interrogation than was a uniformed armed forces prisoner of war. The agents could not claim any rights whatsoever. The shock of arrest so disoriented some agents that they talked freely to save themselves and provided information that was used to the determent of others.

The German security services knew all these conditions and tricks of this trade and were well versed in the methods of ruthlessly breaking the willpower and spirit of secret agents who fell into their hands. Few came out of this ghastly experience alive. Hitler's notorious order was to give short shrift to anyone caught working against him behind the battle fronts in uniform or not.

Double Agents

We know of electorates where voters will change sides for selfish and/or greedy reasons. When anxiety and fear from suppression and brutality are added to this equation, it is not surprising that people change sides. This possibility should have been taken seriously! The Germans knew that some people were susceptible to changing their views and would agree to help the Nazi cause. Some were easy as they already believed in the concept of National Socialism or admired German militarism. Others had no firm view and were open to indoctrination. Others regarded by the Germans as being useful to their cause, were manipulated, blackmailed, or worse. These people became double agents. They were normal citizens, who like mines in a minefield, went undetected until you trod on them. Double agents were a menace who caused the arrest and death of many secret agents and their helpers. Escape lines were very vulnerable to double agent penetration. The so-called Judas Procedures were often included in message transmissions by radio, mouth, or a sign.

These procedures warned whoever was listening to the radio that something was dangerously amiss without causing suspicion or alerting the enemy. Examples were spelling a word incorrectly or adding an extra word or sign, such as carrying a flower or something unusual, so the radio message receiver or agents were warned. Although the messages were received and understood, they were not always believed or followed up on with fatal consequences.

Hans Rauter, writing to a friend in 1942, wrote: "Thanks to sixty death sentences, forty-five of which have been carried out so far, Holland is now a model, orderly, occupied country."

He was mistaken. Secret agents kept coming and were arrested right away. Their codes had come into German hands, and they were picked up nearly on the spot where they landed by parachute. They forced British trained radio operators to work for them so that their characteristic of Morse keying and the use of their secret codes would seem genuine. The SS codenamed this the

Englandspiel, meaning the Game against the English. It was played for a long time without London being aware of it. It was fatal for many secret agents and their helpers.

There were many unreported fatal endings to subversive actions, which made the Netherlands a very dangerous place for these sorts of capers against the German Reich.

Homecoming

May 16, 1940

The way things worked out, I never saw Mr. and Mrs. Smit again. It was fifty-five years later that I saw the town of Den Helder again and it was at least double in size.

I was just twenty years of age, had come to the end of an era in my life, and the world around me was in chaos! My plan was to go home where I spent school holidays for the last three years; the place where my family lived, a safe haven or sanctuary. But above all, it was where my mother was.

The Family de Vries, Jan and Truus, were very understanding and heard me out. I was assured that, if I were willing to help them on the farm, they had no objection to my staying with them. Farm life not only meant early hours and hard work, but also companionship and they would have someone to talk to. I told them that it was my plan to go home to The Hague and needed to contact my parents by phone. We tried phoning them but were unsuccessful.

May 17, 1940

Today we got through to my parents by phone. They were delighted to hear my voice and had a thousand questions. I explained my fear of what the Germans may do to me if I fell into their hands, so I had to wait to see how the Germans were reacting before moving on the railway or roads. They agreed and warned me to be careful.

The rest of the day was spent helping in the stable. At supper time, I told them I planned to walk to The Hague along the coastline. I would start from Camperduin and try to reach Scheveningen. It would probably take three or four days. Jan de Vries told me he had a better idea. One of his friends worked for the Farmers Cooperative and often drove a large truck of farm products to Alkmaar. With a bit of luck, he would agree to drop me off at the coast near Edmondaan Zee saving fifteen to twenty Km of the approximately seventy to eighty Km from Camperduin. That sounded very good.

38

Jan took me to his friend who agreed to do it if I would wait one more week. I worked in the farm that week. I worked in the stable which was hard work that I was not used to, but it did not kill me, and I probably became a better man for it.

Friday, May 24, 1940

On Friday morning, Mr. de Vries friend and I went to Middendorp to meet and boarded the truck. I forget this man's name, so I'll call him Peter, Piet in Dutch. I packed a rucksack with a rolled-up blanket, a supply of sandwiches and a flask of coffee all provided by the Family de Vries. I started my trip with Peter to Alkmaar and the coast.

Piet was a humorous man, full of jokes and laughter and a pleasure to be with him. He was a real tonic and was, as the saying goes: a laugh a minute. He was just what I needed. We had no trouble and saw no Germans. He dropped me outside the door of a friend of his near Egmondaan Zee where I was received cordially.

They gave me a nice lunch, told me that the coast was not far away and gave me directions.

Walking along the seashore on the hard, wet sand was a pleasure with a cool breeze blowing, sometimes with long stretches empty of people and at other times with people enjoying the sun and a swim. Food and coffee were always for sale.

The next major obstacle was the harbor of IJmuiden with its large locks for seagoing vessels. It would probably be occupied by the German army or navy, so I got off the beach at Wijkaan Zee. I had to get myself from Wijkaan Zee and around IJmuiden via Velsen. On my walk along the seashore I swam from time to time washed myself, so I felt refreshed.

After a stiff walk, I went inland and by now, probably had a socially unacceptable odor! As Shakespeare said, "That which we call a rose by any other name would smell as sweet."

I came to a little roadside restaurant just before I reached Velsen. It had a parking area with lorries and vans parked there. It looked like a transport riders' watering hole. The place was full. I asked one chap sitting alone at a table if I could join him. With his mouth full, he pointed his fork to an empty seat in front of him.

I put my rucksack down and asked him if he would be so kind as to watch it. Again, with his fork gave me the okay sign. I went to the counter to order my food and drink, paid for it, and joined my newly acquired friend.

The first words he spoke were, "You are on the run, aren't you? You are not the only one and you all look and smell the same! All these poor chaps from the army and navy that do not want to become prisoners of war. Where are you going? Maybe I can help you."

I was so perplexed by this "how-do-you-do," that I sat there tongue-tied for a while. I lifted my left arm and sniffed my armpit, then my right arm and sniffed then shrugged my shoulders and said: "You got me, you're right; I'm going to The Hague"

I must have looked like I was going to run then because he said, "Take it easy, here we are all on your side—eat first and rest."

So I ate while my friend went round to some tables. He came back and said, "You're out of luck, they're all going north. I am a builder and subcontractor laying parquet and lino floors and I'm returning to Haarlem. You can have a bath at my place and then I'll take you to the station. Don't be scared anymore. The German High Command just declared that all the Netherlands forces can go home. We seem to be their Arian blood-brothers, so relax!"

To cut the story short, it was not long after that incident in Velsen that I rang the doorbell at Beeklaan 450 in The Hague. I was home at last. I phoned my parents from the station, so they expected me. We were all delighted and thrilled to be together again and we had plenty to talk about. To crown it all, my mother had prepared a delicious meal of fried rice, the Indonesian nasigoreng for me. (Note: I was born on the island of Java and spent my first ten years there.)

I borrowed some clothes from my twin brother and my father, so I could get out of my filthy clothes, which needed a good wash! I had a bath and talked with my family until bedtime. That night I slept badly. My brain was doing overtime and had bad dreams. In the middle of the night, my father came to my bedroom and woke me as I was shouting in my dream. The next morning, I phoned the Family Smit in Den Helder to tell them that I was home safe and to thank them for all they did for me. Mr. Smit then told me that his daughter Annie was looking for a job in or near The Hague, as Den Helder had become a ghost town. All Dutch naval activity had stopped and was taken over by the Germans. He said that Annie was a dressmaker, a good cook and had finished high school. I told him that my family could probably help, and I would let him know. I phoned the Family de Vries to tell them that I was home safely and to thank them for what they did for me. My clothes and belongings were still with them, and I had their clothes and camping gear, so we decided to pack the things and send them to each other by a Parcel Service, and that I would pay for it all. After approximately two weeks I had all my belongings back.

Three or four weeks later, we found a job vacancy for Annie as a housekeeper in a hospital north of The Hague near Valkenburg. I phoned Annie in Den Helder and told her to apply for it giving her all the details. In the meantime, she could stay with us in The Hague which she did. Later she got the job and seemed to like it.

Within six months, she married the owner of a local baker's shop and I never saw or spoke to her again. It was for the best, as I missed her very much.

Life is a Folly

If you live long enough nothing is surprising. There are men with a purpose who are efficient, well trained, well equipped and fit for one purpose only: "to make more men die for their country than they do for their own." Is that not a good way to win a war? Of course; That was how the victorious German forces looked and behaved. They were well groomed, especially their officers in tailored uniforms and shining riding boots; well behaved, charming and cultured. Even their soldiers and sailors would get up for the elderly and women in trains and trams who could not find a seat and were standing in the aisle.

Their civil administration, also in uniform, swung into operation quickly and efficiently. They took control of governmental functions and directed those functions that supported the German war effort. They left management in Dutch hands, under their control, until proven unreliable or counter to their war-effort. God help those who impeded or obstructed the system. The Germans regarded this as sabotage, a war crime with serious consequences.

The Germans quickly became part of daily life; some admired them, others took them for granted and still others hated them deeply. It was a very dangerous mix. You never knew who was pro NAZI. This was the backdrop to my situation in June 1940. I did not want to be press ganged into forced labor in the German coastal merchant navy, harbor activities, or any such occupations. I decided to keep well away from the German controlled labor bureaus. My parents suggested that I take up bookkeeping by finding a teacher to instruct me on how to keep books of account and possibly gain a recognized qualification. From their church, they found a Mr. Kampen who would accept me as his pupil. Mr. Kampen was a small elderly gentleman who lived on his own in a small flat near us. He kept books of account of some of the shops near us and consulted businesses on filling in tax returns. He was a very kind person who tried to teach me with infinite patience. But the truth was that I was simply not cut out for this kind of work. As things stood, there was nothing else that I could do at this time and in the world we found ourselves. I tried for a while, but eventually gave up, thanked Mr. Kampen, paid him his due and phoned my friends Jan and Truus de Vries on their farm in the Wieringermeer Polder to ask them if I could come back and work for them as a farmhand. They agreed so I packed my bag, including my books on bookkeeping, said goodbye to my shocked parents and went to the railway station of The Hague.

I soon found out that rail traffic for civilians was erratic as German forces movement of men and material took precedence. The station was full of German forces and public train times were constantly readjusted. I finally found standing space on a train going north to Alkmaar, where, I was told I could get to my destination by train or bus.

I was satisfied as I was going in the right direction. I could work out something at a later stage. Apart from the normal railway station stops, our train was sidetracked twice to allow priority freight trains to pass. Eventually we arrived at Alkmaar station at 22:30. It was dark, raining softly, and I was tired and hungry in a sleepy town with empty streets. After searching, I found an all-night café frequented by lorry drivers. I flopped down, had something to eat and drink and fell asleep in my chair with my head on my hands. I woke up about 02:00 in the morning stiff as a plank. The waitress, who cleared my table had kindly let me sleep. She came over, put down a lovely steaming hot cup of coffee (coffee was still available), sat down opposite me and asked if I was all right. I told her that I was on my way to a farm near Slootdorp.

"I don't know where that is, dear, but around five o'clock drivers come in for their breakfast. Some of them are going to Friesland or Groningen via the Afsluitdijk and would probably give you a lift to a point near where you want to go."

True to her word, the first driver came in at 04:30. With a kind word from the waitress, came over to my table to tell me that he would drop me off near Slootdorp. He did and after a five km walk

I arrived at the farm of Jan and Truus de Vries. They welcomed me with open arms and a bed where I disappeared into a deep dreamless sleep.

It was now late August 1940. I worked hard at the farm and found peace at last.

Reflection

With my peaceful existence at the farm, I was free of the interference and turmoil war caused. I slept in a nice warm bed not wanting to get up in the morning, I lived a sedentary trance which I had to get out of! The hard work at the farm was an opiate or an escape to a quiet peaceful and wholesome bolt hole where I could come to terms with my plight and from which I could hopefully make a new beginning.

I realized that I was at a turning point. A decision had to be made to change matters or at least look around to see what crazy war had to offer that would suit my makeup, i.e. my abilities, personality, and character. I did not want to go to the German controlled labor department, so I scanned the advertisements in the newspapers. This was a first step in the right direction and it worked!

The Earl's Hedgerow

Beginning May 6, 1941, I was employed by the Municipal Secretariat of 'sGravenhage as a temporary Civil Servant with the Registrar of Population, Electioneering and Civic Registry. I was charged with issuing identity documents and with the details to produce and complete them.

For English speaking people, the city of The Hague, of South Holland, has an abbreviated Dutch name, *Den Haag* from the very old historic name *Die* Haghe. Its present official name is 'sGravenhage. That translates into English as *The Earl's Hedgerow* or simply *The Hague*.

This job was advertised in a national newspaper, so I applied for it but did not expect that it would come to anything. A glimmer of hope came in the middle of March when the post brought a personal interview in The Hague. The job was offered, and I was asked to start on May 6, 1941. This gave me time to settle my affairs and return to my parent's home, where my room was still available. I left the farm in the middle of December 1940, expressing my heartfelt gratitude to Jan and Truus de Fries. They, to my astonishment, gave me a sack full of farm products to take to my parents.

While on the farm the world passed me by. But Jan and Truus knew that farm products were growing scarce for town and city people. Needless to say, my mother was delighted with this gift. It was the first time I realized what this war was doing to the food supply and learned from others that the Germans controlled the food distribution and gave priority to feeding their forces.

Coming back to city life, I noticed the German forces were everywhere. They foisted restrictions on the population; such as the identity documents which I was producing and issuing. Entry was forbidden entry into prohibited military areas, a coastal strip cutting right through Scheveningen and the western parts of The Hague, stretching from Den Helder to Normandy and beyond without an Ausweis (permit).

I spent Christmas 1940 with my parents, my twin brother Maarten and my sister Willy. She is slightly older and prefers to be called Wil. She regards that as more dignified, but I always called her Willy which she tolerated. The five of us had a peaceful Christmas; church in the morning, a restful afternoon with tea and cake; ending the day with a nice supper.

I made contact again with old friends and acquaintances and with the social and entertainment establishments of The Hague. To me, a country bumpkin, they were an absolute delight. One of these places was a dancing club, called Gaillard in the Laan van Meerdervoort. I joined to learn the latest steps and become more sociably acceptable. For its time it was a modern, joyous and lively club with a patient woman instructor and male dance master getting my clumsy feet to do the light fantastic for dances such as the waltz, foxtrot, quickstep and tango; it was accompanied by amplified gramophone music. Dance evenings with a band on Saturday gave us experience with our partners and other students. It was an exciting and lively club; well known among the young at heart in The Hague. I made many new friends. (Who said there was a war on? What war?)

Time flew by until May 5th. Before going to bed I selected and made ready clothes suitable the look of a real civil servant.

The next morning, a crowd of some one hundred people waited at the offices of the Municipal Secretariat in the Goudenregenstraat 36 for the doors to be opened and to be ushered in.

A uniformed caretaker opened the doors and requested that we allow the regular civil servants to enter first. To my surprise a sizeable crowd of young men remained. Our papers were checked before we were lead into a huge hall with a curtained stage at one end. We were asked to sit near the stage for the Registrar who would address us soon. In the meantime, each of us received papers related to the job we were to do. It was very impressive. Everyone received a municipal identity-card which allowed us to enter this building. We signed a declaration to not divulge the things we were going to be taught or wrongfully misuse or defraud this Identity Document System. It looked very legal and official making us feel as if we had joined a secret society or brotherhood.

After these preliminaries, the stage filled with officials and police officers. Soon we were asked to settle down and pay attention to the Registrar. He addressed us with well-chosen and refined words expressing the importance of what we were going to do.

The next person to address us was a police officer. He told us that the police were going to instruct us in how to take fingerprints, after which we were given morning coffee and cake. After this we were divided into alphabetic groups; A to D, E to G, and so on. It had nothing to do with the first letter of our family names but with the family names of the citizens who were to receive their identity document. Instructors came in carrying boards with the alphabetic groupings and joined our allotted group. After meeting our instructor, we were told that we could go home and report the next morning to start our training.

Each alphabetic group consisted of one, two, three, or more persons depending on how many citizens' family name began with a particular letter; such as the name Jansen with many under the letter J. The next morning the hall was cleared of all theatre chairs. It was divided into rectangular spaces, one for each alphabetic group. Inside each space were two tables, side by side, with enough chairs to seat a group and their instructor. The tables had all the tools, bits and pieces necessary to do our job, such as; a small portable metal safe that held various stamps and a stamp pad, two bottles with special ink, writing pens, special seals, blank identity documents and other small implements. On the tables were glass plates with rubber ink rollers and thick black ink for taking fingerprints, and various official blank registry forms and documents. The next four days were devoted to explaining every form, document, inks and seals and how to use them.

The police showed us how to take fingerprints of all ten fingers and the palm of the hands, and explained what made a good, bad or useless print and why. We did all these things ourselves and

produced identity documents for each other, our instructors and municipal staff. Each product had to be approved by an instructor and police officer before they were officially handed out.

I proudly showed my identity document to my family. They were dubious about my doing this work as it reeked of German involvement, which it was. Although I never saw a German uniform near our work, the feeling was that this whole scheme was ordered by Dr. SeyssInquart, the Reichskommisar.

TRANSLATION OF OVERLEAF DOCUMENT
(PAGE 29)

The Burgomaster (Mayor) of The Hague

declares that, until further notice, he has assigned *C.Gutteling*
as an official, empowered to do the necessary essentials for the entry and
completion, drawing up and issuance of Identity Cards, as well as other
related activities.

  The Hague   **The Burgomaster (Mayor) above mentioned.**
  14 May 1941   **Signed**

Corr.no.77062, Afd.B.V.B.

DE BURGEMEESTER VAN 'S-GRAVENHAGE,

verklaart, dat hij   C.GUTTELING

tot wederopzegging heeft aangewezen als ambtenaar, gemachtigd om namens

hem het noodige ter zake van het in- of aanvullen, opmaken en uitreiken

van Persoonsbewijzen, zoomede de andere daarmede verband houdende werkzaam-

heden, te verrichten.

's-Gravenhage,   De Burgemeester voornoemd,

14 Mei 1941.

C.L.van der Bilk

Weth.wnd.Burg.

Who Needs a Hole in His Head?

Who needs a hole in his head? Certainly not Arie Huiser, who looked at me fiercely and whispered: "Tip, I need you like a hole in my head; get out of here!"

That was some plain speaking, so I quietly left the storeroom. All I wanted from Arie was some stamp pad ink for my own use. I later realized how lucky I was in having my request refused as the stores were well guarded by security staff who seemed to be everywhere.

Arie Huiser and I shared a classroom in primary school, we played together in the school yard, and often walked home together. Arie lived in a small flat in the Fahrenheitstraat with his mother and older sister. He never knew his father. His sister was a manicurist and chiropodist with regular clients from whom she made the money to sustain her small family. Arie worked here at the Municipality, but not as an identity document producer. He was one of our storekeepers. His store kept all the blank documents, inks, seals, and similar items from which we replenished our supplies.

Before starting in the morning, I collected my metal safe box from the store with my signature. Before going home, we completed and signed a request form for items we needed for the next day's work. Some days we would run short of items due to a rush of customers or if we spoiled documents, which was easily done while fingerprinting clumsy customers.

We had to restock from the store by filling in a Request Form and calling a guard or instructor who got it for us. We were not allowed to leave our table while there were customers in the hall.

The hall was well guarded by plain-clothes security guards. When we needed to go to the toilet, we locked up our stamps and seals and caught the eye of one of the guards. He would stand by your table until you returned.

I describe this in detail to show that everything was organized to the tenth degree to ensure maximum security. Our daily tasks started at 08:45 when the loudspeaker would tell us to sit at our table in readiness for our customers of the day.

At exactly 09:00, the outside doors were opened to the public. Ushers told them how to proceed to their allotted table, where they were to sit and hand over the postcard which they had received. The details were checked with them orally, such as: "Are you so-and-so, and so on." We opened a book which held all the details the Municipal Registry had on all persons in our alphabetic group. After we found the particulars on the person in front of us, we interrogated that person until we were satisfied with his or her true identity. If we were not satisfied, we called one of the security guards who lead that person away. Our customers were required to bring two passport photos, a birth certificate, a marriage certificate if applicable, a passport, or other documents to substantiate their identity, and tell us their address and their religion.

When we needed assistance with the interpretation or technicalities of documents, we could call on instructors to assist us. Then we took prints of all ten fingers and the palm of both hands and placed these on a special form. Then we put the thumbprint of the right or left hand, depending on their dexterity, onto their identity document. We sealed the thumbprint with a special translucent, chemically sensitive seal, which discolored if tampered with. After this, we gave them cleaning fluid and a small towel to clean the ink off their hands.

One of their passport photos was put onto the identity document and stamped. The other photo was put onto their fingerprint form for safekeeping in the Municipal file.

The identity document was completed using special ink to fill in all the personal details. Then it was given to the customer who was escorted off the premises by a security guard.

TRANSLATION OF OVERLEAF DOCUMENT
(PAGE 33)

The Burgomaster (Mayor) of The Hague,
on the grounds of clause 3 of the by-law no. 152 of 1941 from the
"Reichskommissar"(National Governor) of the occupied
Netherlands territory (By-law 1941 - piece 33), the task
performance of the Board of Burgomaster (Mayor) and Aldermen,

In view of the Regulations for Public-functionaries and of the
Regulations for the General Scale-of-Salaries 1936;

Takes note, that

*C.Gutteling, born 8 April 1920, on an annual salary of f1050,- has
been employed as a temporary emergency-official, from 6 May up
to and including 31 December 1941.*

The Hague,
2 January 1942   The Burgomaster (Mayor)
                                          above mentioned,
The Secretary,   *signed*
  signed

This work lasted until December 13, 1941. It was nonstop
production, five days per week. By then nearly every citizen in The
Hague's municipal area had received their Persoonsbewijs or
identity document. A small staff was retained to do the hospitals,
prisons, children who came of age.

On the last day, we were all photographed in one big group of
one hundred and sixty-four persons. This included the storekeepers,
security guards, instructors, and the Registrar and his retinue. No
German uniforms were seen during this whole exercise from May
1941 until we finished.

Corr. no. 88477, Afd. S.Z.

DE BURGEMEESTER VAN 'S-G R A V E N H A G E,
op grond van artikel 3 der Verordening no. 152
van 1941 van den Rijkscommissaris voor het be-
zette Nederlandsche gebied (Verordeningenblad
1941, stuk 33) de taak waarnemende van het College van Burgemeester en Wethouders,

Gelet op het Ambtenarenreglement en op de
Algemeene Salarisverordening 1936;

Neemt aanteekening, dat
C. Gutteling, geboren 8 April 1920, op een
jaarwedde van ƒ 1050,- van 6 Mei
tot en met 31 December 1941 als tijdelijk cri-
sisambtenaar ter Gemeentesecretarie is werk-
zaam geweest.

'-Gravenhage,   De Burgemeester
2 Januari 1942.   voornoemd,

                                                   Wnd.Burg.

De Secretaris,

                    Wnd.Secr.

K 9351, A.Z.A.

Consequences

The nationwide distribution of this Persoonsbewijs or identity document was a powerful tool in the hands of the German security services.

The Jews, to their detriment, were now easily identified.

This identity document was difficult to falsify or reproduce, unless you were well versed in its production. Many tried and botched it; some with fatal consequences. The occupied Netherlands was notorious for its excellent set of identity, permit, and other kinds of documents. This made the work of the English secret services very difficult.

This document's good side was that you could be easily identified, for personal safety, in post offices, banks, and so on.

Note: A historian of the false document section in England once wrote in a typescript report:

> The only way to learn this subject is to grow up with it. This was not only true for forging false papers, but for every other face of the clandestine world, yet the time to grow up with it was unavailable for the British secret service wartime agents. Also, the use of the wrong type of paper or the color of the stamp gave the game away. This subject of clandestine falsification of papers is very tricky. There is nothing more frightening than being challenged by the enemy doubting the correctness of your papers.

Star of David

One day while walking home, a woman overtook me and asked, "Hello Tip, do you remember me?" Without waiting for my answer, she said, "I am Roos, Arie Huisers' sister." (Roos means and is pronounced, rose.) She caught me by surprise; looking at her carefully I said, "Of course Roos, you look a bit older, but still as lovely."

She said she would come to the point quickly and told me that her family was Jewish and asked if I could help them by giving them a non-Jewish identity document. That took me totally by surprise; I never knew they were Jewish. After all, they went to a Calvinist primary school with me. I did some quick thinking; there and then I decided to help them.

Note: By this time, September 6, 1941, all Jews had to wear the yellow Star of David on their outer garments.

I told her that meeting in the street like this was open to observation and could be dangerous if we followed through on this. I suggested she join the Gaillard dance club where we could contact each other in a natural, social setting. She nodded and wished me good day and left. This encounter lasted a few minutes and would have looked as if she had asked me for the time or direction.

I was perplexed: Arie Huiser and his family Jewish? They must be very scared. They did not look or act like Jews and could easily be taken for non-Jews. Helping them would be very tricky and needed to be approached with the greatest of care. Oh well; it was not impossible but quite a challenge, and dangerous!

It took a week before I found her at the dance club and invited her for a drink. Real coffee and tea was replaced by a bad tasting substitute the Germans called ersatz. We got used to it.

Roos told me that Arie had most of the things we needed and could get more if needed to do this good work.

"Listen carefully, Roos. A story of mice will illustrate what I am trying to say. Roos, the second mouse gets the cheese; the first mouse dies in the mousetrap. When you become a suspect, your house becomes a trap. Tell Arie not to keep his contraband where he lives. That is the first place the security boys look. I have to leave my parents' place where I live as I do not want to see them suffer for things I do. And I will not tell them where I'll go. The Germans have a knack for squeezing information out of people. I have decided to help and trust these people, so I have to find a bolt hole where I can work in comparative safety. Come back to the club soon. By then I hope I will be ready to help you. In the meantime, may I have this dance with you?"

While we were dancing she said, "Don't look now and keep dancing. I put something in your jacket pocket."

Oh my God, what next? After the dance, I went to the toilet to see what she put in my jacket pocket and found two small bottles with special ink. Wow, this is dynamite! I was not a trained secret agent with a skilled organization behind me. I felt like a babe in a clandestine jungle, fumbling to do the best thing.

I went back to the dance hall and Roos was gone. I found my usual dancing partner, Bep van Oosten. I had known her since joining the club as we both joined at nearly at the same time and by now were great pals. "Who is she?" was her first remark. "You were very pally together."

I replied, "She is just a new club member who needs to be shown around."

"And you were the knight in shining armor, I suppose," she replied.

I just gave a shrug and said, "Bep, I want to leave my parents' place and find a cheap place in Scheveningen where I can board or rent. Can you help?" I said Scheveningen which was a suburb of The Hague in the Atlantic Wall, the military security area. It was about fifteen km wide. Some places were off limits to everyone except those with a permit. Permits were given to those who lived there or had business there. A military permit could be a good thing to have. Hitler ordered the Atlantic Wall to be built as a coastal defense against attack from the sea. In its early stages of construction, German forces with massive help from forced labor were busy building concrete fortifications, digging a wide anti-tank trench across town with one km wide mine fields along the coast.

Two days later Bep phoned to say that she had found me a place. Could I come and see her at home? She gave me her address in Scheveningen. I went there as soon as I had the time and was introduced to her parents and younger sister. They lived just a block away behind the Oude Scheveningse Kerk near the harbor area.

Bep's father told me that a large attic was on the third floor above them. It had been partially converted into a two-room flat where an old friend of theirs lived very simply. He could use some income from a single boarder who was not too demanding. I agreed to look. He took me there where I met Mr. van Hasselt, who asked me to call him Willem. He had a wrinkled face topped by long grey hair. He was clean shaven, had a kind face, an easy smile and speech and mannerisms that were cultured and pleasant. He showed us a small lounge and two bedrooms. One was his; the other had an empty bed and mattress, a table and chair in it. I had to find my own bed linen and blankets, make my bed and keep my bedroom clean. He showed me a small bathroom and separate toilet. His flat occupied three quarters of the attic space; the other quarter was empty and clean. All woodwork was painted white. Overall his place and attic looked clean. This was a perfect bolt hole. I had plenty of space to do my clandestine work and hide the bits and pieces required for the job under the eaves. I had to make a plan and do some carpentry for the eaves.

He offered tea but Bep 's father invited us all down to his place where his wife made us pancakes. Six of us; Bep's family and Willem and I sat around a table having tea and pancakes with sugar, a real treat in wartime scarcity.

I learned that Willem van Hasselt had been a high school teacher. He lost his house, wife and daughter in the Rotterdam bombardment and had to live very frugally. I later found out that the Old Church and other people helped him have a decent living.

So, I said, "Willem, it's a deal; I'll take it and move in next weekend."

We shook hands to clinch the deal. Bep's father, Mr. van Oosten, got up and gave the men a jenever and the ladies advokaat.

Back at my parents' place, I went to my sister Willy's room. Willy had always been my confidante. Although she was four years my senior we used to play together, climbing trees, fooling around and having a great time. Now, we were older and more reserved, so I knocked courteously on her door, waited for her "come in" and entered.

She took one look at me and asked, "What is wrong with you; are you all right? You look all shaken or are you in trouble?"

How does one answer such a stream of questions? So I said, "I'm leaving home; how is that for a start?"

That astonished her, but she said calmly, "Go on, out with it."

I told her everything, ending by saying, "I need you to tell Pa and Ma once I've gone, not in detail but enough for them to appreciate that I'm doing it to keep you all out of trouble in case this house is raided. My post will still come here. Would you please keep it for me? I will keep in touch with you. I leave next weekend." (That was in October 1941.)

Learning Curve

I bought sheets, pillowcases, warm blankets, and a pillow which I took to Willem van Hasselt's flat. He was home and we had a long chat about general everyday things and the war. He asked what I did for a living. I told him, and he reacted with raised eyebrows, saying, "Why would you help the bloody Krauts? Are you a National Socialist? If you are, then I would like you to leave right now!"

I told him why I needed his flat. If it did not suit him I understood as things could become hazardous.

His mouth rounded to a big "Wo-o-ow!" then said, "You're a man after my own heart. If I can help, please ask me!"

That settled that; which was a great relief. We could work things out later. He was all smiles now and expressed regret at not having a drink in the flat.

The weekend came, and I settled into my bedroom with my few belongings. To my great surprise I found that Willem had already made a small secret hideout under the eaves. He was very keen to help whenever he could and wanted to know how I was going to feed myself. He added that he had his evening meals with various friends in the neighborhood, but often with the van Oosten family. I told him not to bother anyone on my behalf. I could fend for myself with a grocery shop and a café nearby.

I phoned Roos Huiser, told her that I had a place away from home and was ready to help them. I suggested that we meet at the club on Monday. She agreed, and we met in the bar.

We thought that the tricky part would be finger printing away from where we lived. She suggested that she approach another Jewish family who owned a hardware shop, managed and run by a non-Jew. Perhaps we could operate in one of their storerooms. She gave me an envelope with a supply of blank forms and documents, seals, a rubber printing ink roller and a tube of printing ink; all wrapped in brown paper in a shopping bag. I told her that we needed a piece of thick glass about twenty cm by six cm which the hardware shop could cut for us. After this, I left Roos at the club and rushed back to the flat.

It worked out as we planned, except I now had four more customers in the family who owned the hardware store. I pleaded with them not to tell other Jewish people or try to rush things. We had just started and had to find our footing. When everything was in place the process went as follows: Roos Huiser, my first customer, would come to the hardware shop near closing time. When all customers left, she would go to the storeroom where I waited.

If there were customers in the shop, she would wait until they left. I had everything ready and immediately started putting her finger and handprints onto a blank form and the new identity document. I told her that I needed her existing identity document, for one night, to copy the details; and that she should not venture outside once she arrived back home.

Then I hid the fingerprinting paraphernalia in a cunningly constructed hiding place in the store between all sorts of hardware and waited until the shop closed for the night. In a small office in the store, which could be blacked out and made lightproof with curtains, I switched on a strong desk light. I worked on the form and identity document. I used special ink to copy the details from the old to the new documents. In the space for religion I wrote Protestant, Calvinist, or Catholic as requested.

The tricky part was next—the seal, the passport photo and their stamps. First, I stuck a special translucent and chemically sensitive seal over the thumbprint on the new identity document. On a small gas burner, I hardboiled an egg, peeled it and rolled this egg, still warm and moist, over the official stamp on the old document. This picked up the image from the original stamp. Rolling the egg onto the new document transferred a faint copy of the original stamp, which I then touched up with a fine touch up pen using special stamp-pad ink. It made it look real and like the original. It was tricky but effective, requiring many hours of experimenting and training oneself ad nauseam. This trick would only work if the stamp or signature was not too old and dried out; but it was worth a try. (See the Notes at the end of this chapter.)

With that the job was done except for drying and final inspection.

The new identity document and official form for filing were carefully inspected with a magnifying glass. If I was not satisfied and could not correct it the whole process was repeated.

I put the new identity document into an official Municipal envelope and took it to the address of the owner of the document and put it into the letterbox. I did this either that night or in the next morning if a curfew prevented me from going out at night.

All went well with the Huisers' documents. When Arie's turn came I decided to teach him how it was done in all its details, so he could take over if it became necessary. He agreed and together we spent nearly a whole Saturday night going over every detail until he did his own identity document to my satisfaction. I told him the whole exercise must not attract any public attention: that is the comings and goings must look natural. In addition, great attention must be made to cleanup and stow away all the paraphernalia. And make doubly sure that no telltale bits, pieces, spots or marks were left after the job. The slightest slip up could be fatal. Customers were to be told in no uncertain terms that they follow orders.

All this went nicely until early December 1941. My sister Willy gave me a letter addressed to me from the Department of Trade, Industry and Shipping telling me that my employment with the Municipality was ending on December 31, 1941. I was to present myself for further employment with the Bureau for the Metalworking Industry.

What next? I showed the letter to Arie and Roos and told them this might end what I was doing for them. They must make sure that they knew everything about our secret activities so that they could continue with this clandestine endeavor. I spent nights with Arie in the hardware storeroom. I gave him all the forms, document, bits and pieces that I had hidden in Willem's flat and wished them well. I never saw Roos in Gaillard again.

Notes: When I learned to do hardboiled egg copying, the peeled egg could deposit or transfer more than one copy; it becomes fainter with every copy. This made a skill exercise in enhancing copies with a drawing pen or touch up brush and special ink, until it looked real. One egg could be used many times over if it was cleaned and rolled into the fluid that dripped from the egg when peeling.

The old copying system was based on using a layer of gelatin rolled with a certain chemical. The sheet to be copied was then placed on this jelly base and rolled with a rubber roller. This left a copy of the script on the jelly. This was inked for making copies. Copying machines were developed using a drum instead of a layer of jelly. The boiled egg was a miniature drum.

Never a Dull Moment

The turn of 1942 became the watershed in my life. What was going to happen would have been hard to guess. As ordered, I reported myself to the Bureau for the Metal Working Industry in the Riouwstraat in The Hague. I was told to start work on January 21, 1942, for a probation period of one month. After that I would be further advised. I was also medically examined and tested for hearing and seeing. The reasons were not known to me, but it frightened me as this Bureau was part of the German controlled Labor Department.

It soon became clear what we had to do. The German Commissioner had ordered that all brass, copper, bronze, and such like articles were to be handed in at gathering places. My job, at one of the gathering places near the Municipal head office was to receive these items and sort them into large heaps for collection by lorries. They were ultimately melted down for the armament industry. We took verbal abuse and sneers from the public as we worked hard to keep up with the stream of metal that came for processing for producing weapons.

In middle February, my employment was extended for an indefinite period, which did not suit me. It was not only hard work but shameful and humiliating to deprive people of their proud possessions. I was looking for a way out, but how?

Because of my previous employment with officially processing and issuing identity documents and clandestinely helping creating falsified identity document, I met many likeminded people. A timid sort of embryonic resistance movement came into being. We started slowly, probing and investigating each other carefully. I was lucky that I was not caught or reported. However, you learn fast when other people are arrested to your left and right.

During this time, I was introduced by chance or intentionally to Anton Bernard Schrader. He was known by his call name Tonnie (Tony in English). He was approximately twenty-five years old, small and slender, with black hair, dark brown eyes, and clean shaven. He had a shy appearance, was well spoken, well dressed and a qualified engineer. Tonnie was the Acting Head of the Bureau for Raw materials of the Government Bureau for the Food Supply in Wartime. It was an influential and important post which made him suspect of being a Nazi sympathizer; then his name Schrader was similar to Schreider, the Sturmbannfurer of the Sipo or Sicherheits policei.

Tonnie had the use of an official car, a very rare commodity in wartime as gasoline was heavily rationed and nearly unobtainable to Dutch people. He never used his official car in private life. He always used the trams or walked. I was suspicious and discussed Tonnie with my sister Willy. To my surprise, she knew all about him and told me not to worry. He most probably could help or advise me; this was a great relief to me.

One day, I went to his upstairs flat in the Obrechtstraat behind the tram 11 stop on the Conradkade. He was at home and kindly invited me to come in as if he expected me. (I found out, much later that my sister had done some clandestine work for him.)

I explained my plight and asked if he could help. He said that he might be able to assist me if I would do something for a good cause. I agreed. He replied that, it would be appreciated, if I would go to Hamburg with a river tug. Wow! How is that for an introduction? Go to Germany, to one of its main naval harbors and dockyards, a top security area. Straight into the lion's den so to speak.

I swallowed twice and said, "Okay what do you want me to do?" I'm not sure if I was brave mad or just stupid?

I was to learn where and how the Germans degaussed their small metal-hulled ships to make them immune from their magnetic sea mines. As Tonnie's Bureau for Raw Materials used river and canal shipping, it was comparatively easy for him to get me a job on a river craft, such as a river tug. A river tug was an ideal platform for spying activities as they moved around harbors for all sorts of jobs. My orders would come from the German Labor Department.

At the same time, this got me off the hook on my present metal gathering job. (Was I jumping from the frying pan into the fire?)

Historical Note:

The Germans started using magnetic sea-mines in September 3, 1939, at the beginning of the war with Britain. This weapon was unknown to the rest of the world. Magnetic mines played havoc with British coastal shipping. They were dropped by parachute at night and became a real nightmare as no remedy was available. It was soon discovered that wooden hulled craft appeared immune to the devices that lay on the bottom of the sea or were embedded in the mud.

In November 1939, a metal container looking like a mine landed on the mud flats at Shoeburyness in the Thames Estuary and was visible at low tide. It was important to get to this object before high tide set in. Lieutenant Commander John Ouvry courageously defused the mine and it gave up its secrets. It became clear to the backroom boys that metal-hulled ships were being degaussed by neutralizing a ship's magnetic field and immunizing the mine's trigger mechanism. Special electrical equipment had to be designed. Ships were now degaussed by fitting a heavy electrical cable around the ship's hull and passing a heavy current from a power generator through it. This extra equipment could be installed on larger ships, but small craft lacked room for extra gear. British electrical engineers worked out a method to degauss smaller craft by passing them through a large electrical coil. But this method had to be repeated from time to time as the craft slowly lost its immunity. The question asked was: How and where did the Germans degauss their small, metal, hull craft so these installations could be destroyed? This is where I came into this tale!

If *it* looks like a duck, swims like a duck and quacks like a duck, one cannot blame the ducks if they think it is a duck.

Clandestine activities require that you blend in with the background and fit sociably with others who are similar. In The

other words you get sociably camouflaged! When race came into question then we, Niederländers, were honorary members or Ehren mitglieden des Volk; supposedly Deutschfreundlich. So I went for it and used this sentiment. When you accept that The Netherlands was not suitable for blazing gun actions for the simple reasons that German forces could easily out blaze you; it was difficult to get away after a fight and the Germans took cruel revenge and made cold blooded reprisals on civilian populations. What remained were clandestine actions: sabotaging, destroying, or spying with subtle disguises which was just as harrowing and dangerous. It is difficult to get used to as it requires you to change yourself and to be constantly aware of the dangerous situation you are in.

Tonnie Schrader and I were on two different levels of the German society; Tonnie was a top Manager in the CivilService with his office in Lange Voorhout 10, the ministerial government area in The Hague and with an official car. I was on the level of a laborer.

TRANSLATION OF OVERLEAF DOCUMENT
(PAGE 43)

The Hague, *21 April 1942.-*
Mr. C. Gutteling
Jur. Kokstraat 268
Scheveningen

With reference to your letter dated 20 April last, I inform you, that I am in agreement that you may already leave your employment with this Bureau as from 1 May 1942.

Bureau for the Metalworking Industry
The Director
signed

We required the right type of camouflage to do our clandestine work. We were different in nature. We had to be careful not to be seen together often. Things had to be handled in a roundabout manner.

DEPARTEMENT VAN HANDEL, NIJVERHEID EN SCHEEPVAART
BUREAU VOOR DE METALEN-VERWERKENDE INDUSTRIE
SECTIE VAN HET RIJKSBUREAU VOOR VERWERKENDE INDUSTRIEËN

Telefoonnummer 557530 t/m 39   'S-GRAVENHAGE, 21 April 1942.-
Interl. Letters L.L.L   RIOUWSTRAAT 174—186
Telegramadres Rijkametallum
Gironummer 100742

Brieven uitsluitend te richten aan het
Bureau voor de Met.-Verw. Industrie   Den Heer C.Gutteling,
en niet aan personen.
                                              Jur. Kokstraat 268,
Gelieve bij beantwoording van dit
schrijven Uw eventueel inschrijvings-   Scheveningen.-
nummer bij ons Bureau te vermelden
en tevens onze referentie:

     AD/P—LK

          Naar aanleiding van Uw schrijven dd. 20
     April j.l. bericht ik U, er mede accoord te gaan,
     dat U reeds met ingang van 1 Mei 1942 den dienst
     van dit Bureau verlaat.
          BUREAU VOOR DE METALENVERWERKENDE INDUSTRIE.
                    De Directeur,

     Cop. A/C-JS.

     FE.

     19921 - '42 - K 983

Brazen It Out (Brutaal Volhouden)

On April 16, 1942, the Personnel Manager of the Bureau for the Metalworking Industry and told me orally and in writing that by the Decree for Compulsory Labor Service I had to be registered at the Town Clerk's Office before April 25, 1942. I had to give all the necessary information about myself. I took a copy of my registration papers to the Labor Department. They told me they would make use of my professional training. Therefore, I had to resign from my present employment and report to them as soon as possible. I did what I was told. In reply to my letter of resignation, I received a short notice that agreed to release me by May 1, 1942.

At the Labor Department, I was informed that a river tug, in the harbor of Rotterdam, needed a deck hand who can cook and that the tug was bound for the harbor of Hamburg. It was ready to leave in about a week's time. This river/harbor tug was normally used to pull river barges or assist river/harbor traffic. It had a captain and a crew of three deckhands; one attended to the diesel engine in the machine room and one cooked breakfast and simple meal.

That sounded easy, so I agreed. I was officially registered as willing to serve in Germany and given a Work Certificate with the order to go to an address in Schiedam to be mustered and receive further orders.

I had eight days before I had to report to the captain of the tug *Amelia* in the Spuihaven. I rushed home and pleaded with my mother to teach me how to cook porridge and an eintopfmahl, such as hotchpotch, thick pea-soup, brown beans with bacon and such meals made in one pot or pan. I had one week to learn and make notes. Mum was surprised and wanted to know why. I told her that I could not tell her. She looked at me anxiously and we started straight away, I took copious notes. Thanks to her I regained my self-confidence.

A Labor Department van took me to the tug *Amelia* in the Spuihaven where I reported to Captain Hoekstra, handing over my muster papers. The captain wore an N.S.B. metal badge on his jacket. (N.S.B. stands for National Socialist Association, the Dutch Nazi movement). Captain Hoekstr was tall, well-built, and bronzed by the sun and weather. He had blue, deep looking eyes to search the shore and horizon. It gave him a rugged look—good looking Germanic type man.

It was very thoughtful of him to display his affinity to the Nazis. He, in turn, thought that I was a volunteer, which I was on my papers, to serve the Reich. That sorted things out very quickly and smoothly.

The rest of the crew were ashore which allowed us to have a quiet talk. I told the captain I had never worked on a tug, had no protective and special clothing for this work and needed to be outfitted. He signed and gave me a Purchase Warrant, a list of what to get and an address in Schiedam where I could obtain them.

I came back from my shopping spree with a pair of heavy leatherwork gloves, three blue denim overalls, a pair of heavy leather working boots with steel toecaps, an oilskin coat, a rain hat and a butcher's apron. With my money, I bought a reefer jacket and matching cap for cold weather conditions. On returning I met the other two deck hands; one was Kees (pronounced case), and the other was Jan. They thought my name Tip was good for a laugh but got used to it. Jan looked after the machine room, Kees was responsible for things on deck. Kees was a huge fellow, strong as an ox, with calloused hands as large as coal-shovels.

The captain told him to teach me deck handling and the dangers when working with cables. He was a delightful fellow; as rough and tough as they come, with a heart of gold. He took pride in showing me the ropes, pardon the pun. He had no idea that I had been to a Navigational College. He patiently explained that my new leather gloves and shoes were far too stiff and that I had better soften them with oil or axle grease; otherwise they would chafe my hands and feet. He told me never, if at all possible, to step on a working cable or coil. a cable in use, never to stand in line with a taut towing line, in case breaks and snaps back like a whiplash. In both cases, it would cut you clean in half! His job was to look after the various cables, inspect them, choose the right cable for the job, and report to the captain, who had the final say.

In the meantime, I inspected my cook's galley. It had an oil burning range with two burners, crockery storage, utensil storage, bread bin, pots and pans hanging on hooks, storage space for food and vegetables, a small metal basin with tap for cleaning and washing up, candles and candleholders in case the generator had stopped, and a fire extinguisher. There was no hot water tap. You had to boil water in a kettle or pan.

Before I came on the scene, Jan worked in the galley. He told me where everything was and pointed out that the captain was stickler for a clean galley at all times. I cleaned the drying clothes, floor cloth, and mopped daily!

The captain told us that we were going to Hamburg harbor and the waterways of Schleswig Holstein. We would be stationed in Hamburg and had to get there as soon as possible. Would we have everything on board and ship shape by tomorrow morning at 06:00 when we would refuel at the fuel depot? I learned that food was bought along the waterways we would go through, but make sure that we had enough food on board for two to three days. I did this through the ship chandler who delivered my order that evening. The next morning, we were on underway, at about 08:00 on May 14, 1942.

Our first day was uneventful and interesting. We made our way from Rotterdam along the Oude Maas River, the Beneden and Boven Merwede, and the Waal River, until we met the Rhine River, below Arnhem.

There was little to do after I finished my morning chores. I stared at the passing shore, the expanse of the sky and smelled the tug and felt engine vibrations; the very heartthrob of this power unit.

The captain sat on his high chair in the wheel house with his hands on the steering wheel. When I looked up, he gestured for me to come to the wheelhouse.

"Make us a mug of coffee," said the captain.

When I made the coffee, he said, "Stay here and have a good look how it is done in our waterways. I know from your papers that you are a 4th Mate in the Merchant Navy. I will show you how it is done on our waterways and harbors. We better tell the other deckhands what you are and why I'm teaching you; otherwise they will be jealous." I called Kees and Jan, made mugs of coffee for them while the captain told them. They took it in the right spirit. I think they were a bit awed. From then on, the captain often called me to the wheel-house to have somebody to talk to. He pointed out the different river signs, akin to road traffic signs, included navigational lights at night and how to signal your intentions, especially when overtaking. Later, he let me take the wheel to get the feel for how the tug reacted, especially when approaching a landing and how to handle different currents. He always stayed near the wheel and the machine room telegraph in case I made a mistake. A definite pattern was set for our journey to Hamburg, but that would probably change once we did real work. So far, so good!

PART 3—HAMBURG

September 4th was the beginning
of World War II for the German people.

Hamburg

Hamburg was the second largest city and industrial center in Germany. In spite of the vast extent of the city's outline, only one third was built up. The rest was either industrial, parks, lakes or tree lined canals and the city boasted that it has more bridges than Venice. It originally formed part of Holstein and bears the title of "Free and Hanseatic City."

Note: Hanse was a historic merchant fellowship or guild of merchants. It grew very large and existed for many centuries. It spread along the North Sea coast as far as London and Rotterdam. It ended before 1914 but is still mentioned with great pride. Hanse can mean Militant Multitude.

Hamburg is part of Schleswig-Holstein. With the city of Lubeck on the Baltic, it forms a giant back-to-back industrial area. This northern part of Europe, from Den Helder to the southern part of Denmark was originally Friesian. The islands along this coast are still called the Friesian Islands and includes the Wadden Islands of The Netherlands.

This whole northern area from the Dutch border to the Baltic, i.e. Holstein, Schleswig and Sachsen or Saxon, which is part of the old, defunct, Hannoverian Kingdom where British Royalty originated, was conquered and annexed to the German Second Reich by Prussian General and Reich's Chancellor Otto von Bismarck; Adolf Hitler's predecessor. Hitler thought it necessary to start the Third Reich. The whole northern area of Germany was the Second Reich. When Hitler took over he made it the Third Reich.

How did we get there in our small tug? Regrettably, after sixty-four years my memory lets me down. We arrived at the junction of the Waal and the Rhine rivers turning northward into the River IJssel just before Arnhem. We chugged peacefully past the town of Zutpnen where we turned east into the Twentekanaal in the direction of Hengelo. Before reaching Hengelo, we turned north into the Wiene Almelo Kanaal. At Almelo, we turned east into the Almelo Nordhorn Kanaal and crossed the German border just

before we arrived at Nordhorn. Our papers were checked at the
border and the tug examined before we were given the all right with
a cheerful auf wiedersehen.

Canal trips are very boring as one just sits and watches the
world go by between meals and mugs of tea or coffee, cleaning and
polishing chores.

From time-to-time, I took over the steering of the tug, while
the captain sat in his high bridge chair and read a book or a
newspaper or chatted or snoozed. At Nordhorn we turned into the
Süd-Nord-Kanal, which ran dead straight for miles on end until we
reached Rütenbrokerr where we turned due east into a canal to
Haren and then northeast into the Küstenkanal which took us to the
big Weser River and Bremerhaven.

I tried to keep the boring story of canal systems as short as
possible. The question now arises: "Why did we not go round the
coast from Rotterdam and the Hoek of Holland to Cuxhaven and
Hamburg via the North Sea instead of going through all those
canals?" It was because we could not defend ourselves against air
attacks and avoid mines which could have been laid by air at night.

We were now near the core of the German Navy. The
Wilhelmshaven in the Jadebusen Bay, Cuxhaven at the mouth of the
Elbe River and Hamburg was about sixteen km down the Elbe.
Cuxhaven, at that time was the U-boat harbor from where
submarines departed to seas and oceans to sink ships.

The German Propaganda Ministry had invented a nickname
for these men of the U-boats, the Grey Wolves, as the U-boats were
dark grey in color.

This was exciting. Somewhere near here should be the thing
that I was looking for; the method of degaussing small metal vessels
such as our tug. Maybe we would be degaussed if I was lucky!

We were now in Bremerhafen and turned into a canal system
called the Bederhessa Geeste Hendeler Kanal, which took us to the
Elbe River, east of Cuxhafen and opposite Brunsbüttel across the
Elbe. We now went up the Elbe River and turned southeast. The
Elbe at this point is broad. We picked up our harbor pilot who would

lead us to our berth in Hamburg harbor. Our harbor pilot, a splendid fellow in his harbor-officer's naval uniform, took us near the northern bank of the river, where the shipping channel was. We got our first view of the cranes and derricks of Hamburg harbor when we passed the small town of Wedel. Not long after, we moored at our final destination at the Versmannqua in the Baakenhafen. We had made it and now had to await further orders.

Throughout our voyage from Rotterdam, we were conscious of aircraft activity as we listened in silence to screaming, low flying aircraft, which either just taken off and were gaining height or were landing on airfields near us. We also listened to the deep tonal throb from high-flying bombers, which were followed by faraway rumblings of a bombardment while we were quietly thankful for the distance. We laid up every night, moored at a suitable place as navigational lights on the canals were nearly always out. The navigational signs were difficult to see or just invisible. This meant that we were up early before sunrise to be on our way again as soon as we had the proper visibility.

Kaldenkirchen

As a note of interest, just over the Dutch border at Venlo, there is a small German village called Kaldenkirchen. There was a large concentration camp to receive and temporarily house forced laborers who were sent from the different Labor Departments of the German occupied countries. German industrialists select labor from this camp for their factories or industries. There were Russians, Frenchmen, Polish and Dutch forced laborers in this badly run camp where crime was rampant. They were transported all over Germany to work in factories, mines, towns and cities at all sorts of work. Most workplaces were prime targets for air-attacks and bombing-raids.

Different nationalities received different treatment. The Dutch were the only ones who received a small wage and some privileges such as being allowed to shop or walk around after a twelve-hour work day.

I met some forced-laborers in Hamburg. They were employed by the city council to sweep the streets, or on the docks or shipping yards. Polish forced-laborers had to wear a big red P-badge on their outer garments. The Polish and the Russians were prisoners of war. They were under guard and treated badly.

I later learned that if my work on the tug was not satisfactory, my captain could drop me off at the nearest police station to be sent to this Kaldenkirchen labor camp. That was nice to know! My captain never had it so good after I picked up this bit of information!

Spazieren Gehen (Walk About)

May 22, 1942

Our captain come back on board from a meeting in Hamburg to be briefed by the Harbor Master and Harbor Police and was changing into his working togs when I came into his cabin with a mug of steaming coffee.

"I thought they would" he said, leaving me to guess what he meant and eventually, while combing his hair, he went on, "I thought they would use us as a there-and-back pusher."

That was as clear as mud. I raised my eyebrows and he said, "I don't know, but it looks to me that we'll have to do the dirty work for the navy. Pick up damaged ships and bring them in for repair and there seems to be plenty that are war damaged in their coastal-convoys. That's all I know. Oh yes, we'll get two extra deck hands who, apparently, speak Holländish; let's hope for the best."

"We'll also serve as a taxi for naval personnel and as a standby for larger naval ships when their harbor maneuverability is restricted by a strong wind, current, or by a confined turning space."

We received additional gear during the day; special cables and a hand-held gun to shoot a line over a long distance. The ship's chandler came by to bring us our bread, milk, other staples and to make our acquaintance, as we probably would see him daily. The first of our new crew arrived later in the day showing off his Holländisch, by shouting "*dag*" (good day or hello) from the quay side.

He was, like Kees, a huge brawny fellow with a pleasant face under a dark-grey sailor's-cap, which tried to hide his long, blond hair and blue eyes—a typical Arian. "My name is Fritz and yours?"

Fritz was a good German name and from then on we all got on well with this giant. The other crewmember arrived the next morning. He spoke German until later on when he spoke fluent Nederland's. His name was Ratka. He was about six feet tall, well built with brownish hair and a beautiful set of white teeth. We now had a crew of five and our captain. Because of the small size of our

tug, the three deck-hands Kees, Fritz and Ratka, were to stay in a small hotel Nuestadt part of town while our tug moved to a berth in the Binnenhafen near Neustadt. Hamburg's reputation was tainted by tales of the red-light district, that was a small part of what the city was about. That so called red light area was situated near the Reeperbahn (named after Admiral Reeper and pronounced Raper. This caused smirks among English-speaking foreigners). The red-light areas were in streets that were decently blocked off by two overlapping high walls on each side of the street that prevented anyone seeing inside, they were guarded by police, as well as being under strict control of the Health Department of the City Council. A popular entertainment quarter of Hamburg was the Schanzenviertel, just north of St. Pauli and near two subway stations. The Schanzenviertel had student inns and cheap restaurants with popular entertainment. It was a long walk from our landing
stage.

Another popular area nearer to us was in Ost-West Strasze in Altstadt, where the Gröninger Braukeller was served amber colored Pilsner, a wheat beer, in one-liter stone jugs or stone tankards. We found many shops and bars, snack stands, stalls and restaurants at the Landingsbrücken near our landing-stage where our tug was moored.

The Reeperbahn in St. Pauli was not far from us. It was an avenue with all sorts of entertainment facilities. Cheek-by-jowl stood a cinema next to a restaurant next to a large taproom furnished with long tables surrounded by many chairs. A dais at the end of the room was where an umpa band with brass wind instruments and a set of drums blared out popular national or military tunes. Everyone in the taproom had a merry time singing or listening to singers or a comic and drinking beer out of large beer-mugs or tankards, known as a measure which were served with a considerable head of foam. Waitresses easily carried eight or nine of these heavy tankards at once in both hands. There were also casinos, snack bars, and you-name-it. You saw uniforms of the various forces as well as flocks of families. There was a drawback to all this. It all cost money of which I had little.

What I did was walk and enjoy the sights in beautiful summer days and long evenings. Hamburg is at the same latitude, fifty-three degrees north of the equator, as the English midlands of Liverpool, Manchester, and Sheffield. The city was a joy to behold with beautiful shops, hotels, churches, museums, and other sights and the Alster lakes.

One famous hotel had been in business for a century; the Vier Jahreszeiten was a top-notch luxury hotel besides the Binnenalster Lake. It had three reasonably priced restaurants, but they were more that I could afford. I walked into this hotel, looked around, admired the decor, furniture and antiques, greeted people, and walked out, wishing I could afford it. That's what dreams are made of!

Nearby was the St. Pauli-Elb Tunnel; a clever piece of civil engineering for the 1940s. It ran from the St. PauliLandungsbrücken under the Norderelbe to the Blohm &Vos engineering and ship building yards and wharfs. Two massive lifts, one on each side of the tunnel were large enough to take cars, lorries, and lots of people up and down to the tunnel entrance and exit which, by itself, was a thrill to drop to well below the Elbe riverbed and walk through the tunnel to the other lift. It proved to be a very good bomb shelter during an air-raid.

Der Schlepper (The Tug)

A tug, like a bulldozer, has awesome power at the fingertips of one man who can make this huge machine push, pull, haul or tug in combination. It takes experience and skill to handle the great power and do useful work without causing severe damage. You need to know when and how to apply power, and when to refrain. The terms of reference for a tug-captain, or tug-master, depend on the size of the tug, what work it is designed for, and if it is seagoing or river/harbor bound. The sub-classification is whether the ship to be assisted is under its own power or is without guidance or control or rudderless. His assessment of a situation and the action to be taken is final.

That is why information and communication between the tug and the vessel the tug is helping is crucial. Good radio communication between the captain of the assisted vessel, his pilot (if any), and the tug-master is vital. Harbor tugs are often a ship for all kinds of work, a general utility ship in the hustle and bustle of a large harbor. Like most harbors in Europe facing the Atlantic Ocean, during World War II, Hamburg was deprived of global, international merchant shipping except for coast-vessels. They made the merchant side of the harbor look empty.

Nearly all the work was concentrated on the ships of war of the German Navy; building new types of U-boats; repairing and improving returned U-boats.

This activity included MTBs (motor torpedo boats), destroyers, and shipping repairs in general. The war kept the shipyards very busy, especially the engineering workshops, that made parts from scratch. The work of replacing and repairing was never ending and often parts and units were cannibalized from other ships after a search in other harbors and ship yards. If parts were not available, they were reconstructed. This was why, at the collapse of the Dutch, Belgian and French armies, the British Navy went into harbors to destroy as much as they could and deprive the Germans of their use.

Our tasks were nearly always with the German Navy night and day if necessary. We collected and delivered naval and shipyard personnel with their gear. We worked different watches.

We also had to standby when ships came in and moved around the harbor, to assist in bad weather with high winds, often in support of a pilot in bringing in a vessel up or down the Elbe River.

British and American bombers had Hamburg on a direct, nearly straight line to Berlin and other northern industrial areas. We could hear them high up, daily and night. We heard the distant rumblings of antiaircraft guns and bomb explosions; Our crew members never talked politics or war. We quietly listened to our own thoughts.

Note: *FLAK*, Flieger *Abwehr* Kanone or anti-aircraft gun fire. The acronym *FLAK* was adopted into English. Everyone used FLAK. The V sign with the fingers was invented by the Germans.

We were told that Hamburg was attacked on November 17, 1940, by sixty bombers in a vain attempt to destroy the steelworks and oil-refinery. It started six fires, killed two people and made seven hundred and eighty-six people homeless. We were also told that last year, on March 14, 1941, Blohm & Vos was bombed on two consecutive nights, killing fifty-one persons, with the management offices and a wood storage building destroyed and a submarine in a dock damaged.

Since then, Hamburg, seemed to have been forgotten by the enemy. We heard that some bombers returning home were dropping their bombs for reasons known to the bomber crews. Almost every day, we had antiaircraft sirens wailing, but little happened. This made people nervous and jumpy. Harbor, industrial and shipyard areas had their own warning systems, known jokingly as too late. The Late Warning System was meant to keep everyone working for as long as possible; by being informed by the military that bombing was imminent which obviated false alarms. This was a hair-raising experience when a real conflagration was on top of you and everybody crowded the shelters. Everybody became hardened to these conditions, but it slowly got to some more than to others.

People were assuring one another by saying or singing the popular song: *It will all pass; It will all be over.* People also tended to address nasty remarks to the Engländer or Amerikaner or both.

Note: The British, Welsh, Scots and Irish were all called Engländer in Germany.

Looking back, with the advantage of hindsight, one can question why it was so difficult to find out where small metal vessels were degaussed all you had to do was ask!

I do not want to be pedantic, but during the war, the conditional mood, instinct and conditional reflexes were based on self-preservation. Be careful what you say or do in case it is taken the wrong way by the enemy, his agents, or his sympathizers. The enemy was ruthless! I was eager to question my captain, knowing full well that he was pro-Nazi, but something prevented me from putting my foot on that mine. I worried that he would ask, "What the hell do you want to know that for?"

Instead, I kept my eyes and ears "peeled" as they say in England, i.e. I kept alert and watched; but so far, I had no luck. We were never called to go to the open sea so I took it that we were not considered for a degauss to render the tug immune from magnetic mines. Oh well, have patience! One day our captain put on his best clothes and cap and told me that he had been called by the German Navy to come at once. As it was nearly lunch time, I made him a cheese sandwich and a mug of coffee, brushed down his uniform, cap and shined his shoes.

"You look fine, just like the admiral of the tug fleet," I told him when seeing him off. The other crew members were all ashore as there was no direct call or scheduled work for us. I had the tug to myself and used this time to give the tug a good inspection and found nothing of importance that was of interest. As the tug was in ship-shape order, I stripped to my underpants and found myself a nice little nook to sit in the sun and fell fast asleep until the captain woke me.

I quickly dressed myself and made tea. By the time I brought the captain his tea and cake, he already had changed into his working togs.

Eureka

In mid-September 1942, we had good weather, with thin vapory cirrus clouds in the sky, a bit of a breeze and the world looked just fine. Who said there was a war on? What war? It was all so peaceful that even the seagulls were not airborne but standing one-legged on their favorite boulder preening themselves.

"Don't go away," said the captain as I was looking over the railing. "Hear me out. What do you know about Kiel. Ever been there? You may well have, for the Kieler Week was a well-known sporting and social regatta for boat and yacht races before the war. You might have attended?"

"No sir, not me. I was a merchant navy cadet, the lowest form of life in those quarters," I replied. "Why do you ask?"

"Well sonny-boy, we have to go to Kieler Bay just outside Kiel on the Baltic to pick up a small Dutch coaster from Rotterdam and take her home. She was badly shot up in one of the coastal convoys and is badly in need of repair. Hamburg shipyards have their hands full with work for the German Navy and they have top priority. So, she goes to Schiedam where they have spare capacity. How is that for a surprise?"

"Wow," is all I could say. I had mixed feelings. I hadn't found out what I was looking for and this would prolong my search.

Going back to Holland, even for a short while, was exciting. Maybe they would give us some leave? Getting away from Hamburg would be a break from the anxiety of being under constant threat from air attacks, although so far, we were lucky! Judging from stories that did the rounds in coffee shops and bierstuben, other areas had been hit hard. Although the UFA newsreels in the cinemas showed only newsreels and the news on the radio, were heavily touched by the Propaganda Ministry and gave NAZI propaganda there was still some news. But alas! A big city, with naval ship yards and a large industry like Hamburg, was host to many sailors and travelers who were prophets of woe and bad news.

Three days went past in which the captain had to get all sorts of papers to allow us to travel to the Kieler Bucht; to take on diesel oil, to stock up food, supplies, to organize our stores, and prepare extra bedding for the three crew members who stayed ashore. In that, time we talked to all sorts of people to find out what Kiel was like.

Kielerhafen, we learned, was the home port for armored ships, also known by the Allies as pocket-battleships. They were the Admiral Sheer, Admiral Graf Spee and the Deutschland. We also learned that Hitler had ordered the name of the Deutschland to be changed to Lützow, to prevent a ship bearing the name of the Fatherland the risk of being sunk. He was worried that German moral would suffer. "Wow!" Again; we would go into a prime target area of crucial importance to the enemy, as they undoubtedly wanted to wipe out this lot of pocket-battleships. Kiel was heavily protected by antiaircraft artillery, nearby fighter aircraft squadrons and all sorts of searchlights, radio and radar equipment, and similar equipment. A good witch's brew for a conflagration. However, what we did not know at that time was that these pocket-battleships were not in Kielerhafen or even near it.

Before departing from Hamburg, the captain called us on deck in order to sort out the watch schedule. He explained that the bridge of the tug had a good frontal view, the funnel could be in the way of the backward view, but as the bridge had a roof overhead, there was no view upwards. Consequently, he would need a good lookout watchman on deck all the time. He added that we would be moving into a busy canal as well as into an area, which could become dangerous when air-attacks commenced.

Kiel's harbor area had suffered an air raid in August resulting in very heavy FLAK. We were told that we would probably be called out at very short notice, in which case we would have to get on deck, fully dressed and be ready quickly. The captain instructed me to be his standby on the bridge when I was not required to prepare food and drinks. There were no questions asked and we went on our ways. We progressed down the Elbe towards the North

Sea until we came to Brunsbüttel where we turned right into the Kieler Canal.

The Kieler Canal is the internationally recognized name the Germans call the Nord Ostsee Kanal or North-Baltic Canal. It runs from Brunsbüttel on the Helgoländer Bucht, on the North Sea side, to Heikendort, a suburb of Kiel on the Baltic side. It is approximately one hundred km long, approximately one hundred meters wide and nine meters deep.

Note; After the war this canal was in a very bad condition and was repaired and widened to about one hundred and sixty meters.

It is interesting to note that the work on this canal was started in 1887 and was viewed as being one of the world's major civil engineering projects in line with the Suez and Panama canals.

It opened in 1895. The Kieler Canal shortens the boat-trip from the North Sea to the Baltic by three hundred and fifty nautical miles instead of going round Denmark. It is very popular with thousands of ships and yachts taking roughly eight hours.

We chugged along at a speed of about six knots, the weather was fine and we all enjoyed the scenery. On the first part of the trip we went through Holstein on the North Sea side. This is flat low country, reminiscent of Groningen. The closer we got to a town named Rensburg the area became more undulated and wooded. After about eight hours, we were stopped by a police boat, just before we got to the locks near a small town named Holtenau. A harbor-police officer came on board to tell us that once we were through the sluice-gates we would be in the Kieler Bucht and under strict orders of the German Navy. They required all shipping going into the Bucht to be degaussed. Did I hear that right? Degaussed! Eureka!

The harbor-police-officer was our pilot. He took over from our captain, explaining things as we again went on our way while the police-boat veered away. I stood quietly on the bridge trying to pick up as much as I could of the conversation. My German was not as good as the captain's, but I got the gist of it. I hoped that later on the captain would fill in the bits I missed. Now I could freely talk about it and ask questions.

We went into a side canal that was a lock for smaller craft like ours. It was converted into a degaussing station.

We slowly approached the canal via a wooden bridge that looked like a slim footbridge for passengers as in a railway station from one platform to the other. Our pilot requested the mast be lowered, gave a toot on the ship's siren, and stopped the tug before we came to the bridge. A man dressed in overalls came out of a low building. A bit of back and forth shouting went on between him and our pilot, after which he went back into his building and we heard an engine start. The pilot explained that he had just started up a big generator for the coil. What coil? I could not see one and asked the pilot where the coil was. He replied, "There, in front of us on the bridge over this canal. It goes over the bridge, down the sides. then under the canal and back up again. It goes around a couple of times and makes a large coil. Small vessels like ours go through and are demagnetized or degaussed. The generator feeds the coil with an electric current which sets up a massive magnetic field that neutralizes the magnetism of the vessel and makes it immune from magnetic mines. We moved over a coil coming into this side-canal. It measured the strength of our tug's magnetic field to determine the strength of the magnetic field to be neutralized.

"After we were degaussed by going under the bridge, another coil at the bottom of the canal ensures that we were properly degaussed. If the final check is not satisfactory, we will do it all over again with a stronger electric current." No wonder I never found a degaussing station. It looked so insignificant. In present day terms, it looks simple and easy, but sixty-five years ago it was state-of-the-art in scientific warfare.

This is what I had come for. Now I knew what it looked like and how it worked. As soon as we were back in Holland, I could pass this information together with what I had seen in Hamburg and would still see in the Kieler Bucht to my Resistance group who would transmit the information to England.

The Way Back

We came to the locks and went through together with two coasters. (A coaster is a small ship that goes coastal harbor to coastal harbor. It sails along the coast to trade.) We arrived in the Kieler Bucht with the yacht and motorboat marina on our port side. It was dark and our pilot took us to a quay where we moored for the night. With a friendly aufwiedersehen he disappeared into the night. We were tired and after squaring-the-tug went to our bunks with one of us on guard on the bridge where there was a bench to sit or sleep on.

I awoke at 06:00 to prepare breakfast in the tiny galley. We had a big bowl of steaming hot porridge with black syrup and as much black coffee as we liked.

The next morning, our pilot came back aboard, and we were soon chugging towards our charge, the small war- damaged Dutch coaster. We saw her riding at anchor and came alongside. The captain and Jan climbed on board where a skeleton crew of two Dutchmen with smiling faces awaited them. After a while they came back, and the captain decided that Kees should stay on board the coaster with his kit and personal effects. He was equipped with a walkie talkie, a set of signaling flags and a megaphone to establish two-way communication between the vessels.

We learned that another small harbor tug would follow us to Rotterdam, in case the coaster's rear end needed a push either way in canals as the coaster's rudder was useless at slow speed. The other tug was already coming out of the harbor.

Our group was complete; our own towing tug Amelia, small damaged coaster Doora, followed by the tug Jacoba. The two captains and Kees had a quick pow-wow about communication protocol; radiophones were checked, and we went to our stations. We got cables across as I stayed well clear of the poopdeck where the cable handling was done by Fritz and Jan; both experienced tug hands. Both tugs gave a toot on their siren, indicating that their cable was across to the coaster and secure and that they were ready to take up the slack, so the coaster could weigh anchor. I saw our cable tautening and just as well as the sea current in the bay was already taking hold of the coaster and both tugs controlled her bearing.

Our pilot was on the bridge of the coaster giving orders over the radiophone to both tugs indicating speed by ordering more pull this way or that to control the course of the coaster to get this group back to Kielerhafen and the entrance to the Kieler Canal.

It looked easy, but that's true with specialists, master tradesmen, chef cooks, stunt pilots, and other skilled tradesmen. Once we were back in the locks, we all said a fond farewell to our pilot.

These canals had no side currents like we had in the bay. They were partially protected from weather by land on either side and were generally straight. Our journey home was slow and just as tedious as our journey to Hamburg. We crossed the border into The Netherlands in early October 1942. It felt good to be home again and hear and speak Dutch or Nederland's.

Historical Note

Nine months after we had left Schleswig-Holstein, Hamburg was partly destroyed in four heavy bombardments on July 25, 26, and 28, 1943. It killed fifty-three thousand persons. The number would have been higher, but one million two hundred thousand persons were evacuated beforehand. On December 12, 1943, Bremen, Hamburg and Kiel were bombed by one thousand four hundred and sixty-two American B17 and B24 heavy bomber aircraft in a combined daylight raid. It caused heavy damage and the infamous firestorms in the cities, nearly wiping out the whole industrial area. American losses were over one hundred bombers.

PART 4—ESCAPE

Hide and Seek

Hide-and-Seek is a children's game known to the Dutch as verstoppertje; but when performed out of necessity to hide from a merciless occupation force during wartime, the consequences can be severe or even deadly. It was known as dive down. This was easier said than done. People who gave the sanctuary were dealt with severely; often involving their family and others. It also reduced their wartime food-rations as the non-existent human being had to be fed and maintained. It was not a game and was unpredictably dangerous. The non-existent human being could not be kept locked up. They had to be allowed some exercise in the open for walks and such like. I was well aware of all this as the stories were rife of non-existent human being caught and shot or sent to a concentration camp to do hard-labor. Their poor friends who helped them received the same harsh treatment.

To put this in perspective and explain what it meant to the population; the idyllic period, if there was one with the Germans, ended when the German High Command decreed, on May 23, 1941, that a new government department was to be instituted. The NAD or Labor Service of The Netherlands.

This department would ensure that no able-bodied person was allowed to be out of work! This meant forced labor in the war-effort or weapons industry for anyone without a job including returned soldiers and youngsters who had completed their education.

This affected thousands of people. A panic situation started with people contemplating where to hide. Others contemplated volunteering for all sorts of jobs while the going was good. The churches emphatically condemned voluntary enlistment until they realized that this viewpoint would not stand-up to the might of the occupation authorities. It may do more harm than good and may even be useful. All-in-all, thousands of people went into compulsory labor; most of them into the German war industry which was often under Allied bombing attacks. The families of forced laborer's in The Netherlands were extremely worried. It was known that at times they were fed and treated badly. Relationships between people in labor camps, thrown together by events they were powerless to control or understand affected individuals' lives in a random fashion. People forced to undertake tasks, sometimes dangerous, which they were not equipped.

War or no war, bread had to be baked and brought to the table, so baking had to continue. Before the war, wheat for Dutch bakeries came from the Ukraine as our humid climate was unsuitable for growing the right wheat. When war broke out, we had to use our indigenous wheat which produced poor quality flour resulting in poor quality bread.

Products from warmer climates, such as coffee, cane sugar, tea, tobacco, chocolate and certain fruits, such as bananas, oranges and lemons, stopped coming to the market.

Far more worrying and at times fatal, was the scarcity and stoppage of medicines, such as insulin. Import or production of these products also stopped when the Germans took control of the indigenous chemical factories where products for the German war-effort had top priority.

To make things worse, groups of young people became angry and restless and started to gather into strong-arm squads to fight windmills, such as the Dutch Nazis and related organizations or persons in the name of patriotism. This became serious and the Germans strong arm tactics tried to suppress this. They succeeded only in driving what was left of these groups underground.

This was a very confused and worried country where I returned to with my own worries and vague plans for the future.

On Leave (Met Verlof)

My official leave certificate was given to me in a Labor Department office in the harbor area of Rotterdam and covered a two-week period. I told the authorities that I was on leave from duty in Hamburg. I was never challenged to show it, but the impressive official stamp, with the German eagle perched on a swastika became very useful for our document falsification activities.

I was now in a pickle, a quandary that could lead to my demise if this situation was not handled with the greatest care. I had to get out of my labor service on the German tug. It was scheduled to go back to Hamburg in two to three weeks' time. If I did not turn up for duty at the end of my leave period, I would be a deserter and go on the Gestapo wanted list. I had to move fast!

I contacted my sister, Willy, in The Hague and told her my story. I had to see Tonnie Schrader as soon as possible. With a bit of luck, I met him at his flat the same evening.

I gave a verbal report of my findings in Hamburg, Kieler canal and the degaussing method used by the German Navy and the general situation in Hamburg harbor and its naval shipyards. He made notes and assured me that he would quickly organize a job for me, if possible officially, otherwise he would find a suitable place to go into hiding.

As an alternative, I could try to go back to the farm of Jan and Truus de Vries in the Wieringermeer Polder.

Tonnie was the head of the Government Office for Raw Materials which was closely linked to the Government Office for Food Supply; a set of government services close to the heart of the occupation forces which fed them in The Netherlands. As such, Tonnie had quite a bit of influence. He requested officially through his office that since I had done my stint in Germany and was on leave in The Netherlands, he would appreciate my transfer to his department as my talents were wasted on a river tug. Miracle-of-miracles, the whole thing went through as requested; quickly and without a hitch.

I heard, through my sister Willy, that I was to report to the Department of Labor in The Hague which I did. In due course, I was transferred to the Department of Food Supply and reported for work to the government meal preparation service in Delft on December 1, 1942. That shows very clearly that, it is not what you know, but who you know that counts!

I hung around for the month of November as the so-called factory was not yet completed. I later learned that it was part of a German propaganda stunt to help the poor and needy with Winter Assistance. The little factory that was to prepare meals was part of a large cooking oil factory. Unless one was an admirer of Germany or Nazism, most needy people would not take any advantage of it unless the need was great.

Tonnie had other ideas and plans which he told me about in a session we had in his flat. He had come to the conclusion that times would become very bad in The Netherlands. The availability of raw materials and food supplies was dwindling with the Germans almost stealing, The Netherlands was nearly empty. Who better placed than Tonnie to judge the situation! Getting away from German occupation by any means was on his mind since he had watched the German forces march in.

By chance, Tonnie had come in contact with people who had illegally written, printed and distributed Resistance leaflets. This was the rudimentary beginnings of an underground resistance movement. Being an official position to allocate the supply of gas, he helped some students obtain one hundred liters of this near unobtainable commodity, so they could escape by boat to England. His resolution to help without jeopardizing himself if possible and his influential position was now his aim in life. This was dangerous work where wishful thinking was no help; only hard facts mattered.

Sub-Rosa

Sub-Rosa means under the rose where the rose is the traditional symbol of security. Although; we were not a secret society, a society with secrets, or a band of brothers; we certainly had a strong binding common purpose. We wanted to get away from oppressive German governance as soon as possible by the shortest possible route, i.e. come what may and for better or for worse!

To use army slang; "Don't let the bastards grind you down," was most applicable! Times were getting harder as time went on; laws and dictates became more severe, and living standards deteriorated.

So Tonnie decided to get out, cross the North Sea to England and get his friends to help him execute this plan in the shortest possible time. Tonnie decided how and who would take part in this venture. Since he had the position and the power to allocate and assign basic needs such as road and waterway transport and the allocation of fuel. He foresaw the realization of his plans. Most of his friends like my family and him were colonials born in Netherlands East-India (now Indonesia). Through his contacts, Tonnie got to know Sietse Rienksma, a skipper of a potato carrying barge. He regularly went through the heavily guarded border posts into the Atlantic Wall military coastal fortifications area, commonly known as the forbidden area, with his barge to supply potatoes to the Germans. He had become friendly with the guards. As the saying goes: "Familiarity breeds contempt." But it also breeds attempt on September 1941, Sietse and seven of his friends loaded a motorboat into the barge and took it to Rozenburg not far from the Hoek of Holland, the open sea and well into the military area. Once there, they unloaded the motorboat got away at night to arrive in England the next afternoon leaving his barge behind. This was Sietse's second escape attempt to England after a near disastrous attempt in May of that year. Tonnie helped in both of Sietse's escape attempts by supplying the necessary gas. This was because his close friend, Rudy Burgwall, instrumental in bringing him in contact with

Sietse. All this looks easy when writing about it. In reality, it took a lot of planning, hard work, and anxiety.

Historical Note

Rudy Burgwall became an R.A.F. pilot and was killed over France, declared missing, in August 1944.

The escape of Rudy and Sietse in May 1941 made up Tonnie's mind to organize his own escape. So he set out a plan and decided who his helpers and crew mates would be.

In his influential position, with a car and driver, an extraordinary privilege in wartime, and the necessary security and identity papers, he could move wherever he wished to go. That included the Sperrgebiet along the coast. He had a quiet unpretentious way of delegating and he never noticeably lost his temper.

Kees Koole, also a skipper of a barge, picked up and took possession of Sietse's barge which he had left behind at Rozenburg. Both Sietse and Kees came from Schipluiden, a small town between Rotterdam and Delft, and both knew Tonnie as they both did water-transport assignments for the government. They mainly transported food to the Germans garrisoned in the Sperrgebiet. What a coincidence!

Through the Kees Koole connection, Tonnie increased the number of his helpers, to include Dirk Boonstoppel, a farmer from the Biesbosch southeast of Rotterdam, who could and did put up and hide non-existent human beings and other persons who could assist with boat and engine repairs and supply spare-parts, scarce in war time. Last but not least, he found persons with deep pockets who to help finance his escapades.

This also included the brothers Pier and Jo Meyer, shipbuilders in Leidschendam on the northeast side of The Hague. They worked for the Van Ravensteijn shipyard; Pier was works manager and Jo was a fitter. So far so good; what's more, few if any of them were aware of one another's contribution to what was in progress.

This was truly a sub-rosa symbiosis, whereby one party wants a prohibited product, a seaworthy motorboat, while the other party is willing and capable at a price to supply this product secretly under difficult conditions.

The boats were officially bought in the name of a government organization, such as the North East Polder Workings of the Such-and-Such Government Department, so it was not suspicious at a subsequent German inspection.

Deliberations

Many ordinary common, garden variety things could not be taken at face-value. All had to be examined in detail to avoid danger or unpleasant surprises at the last moment. One of these was the Atlantic Wall or Sperrgebiet. It was in the provinces of South Holland and Zeeland and an Achilles heel of sorts in the form of islands and waterways stretching from the Hoek-of-Holland to the town of Vlissingen near the Belgian border. They were coastal deltas of the Rhine, Meuse, and Scheldt rivers. This whole combined delta area of waterways, islands, inlets, bays, reed fields, sand banks and swampy areas were a headache to the Germans and forced them to place guard ships, operate patrol boats, and position searchlights, as well as build heavy concrete land structures and weapon placements. This could make life extremely difficult and dangerous for escapers, but not impossible. All this military hardware was in place and well manned, but somehow, we thought that in any armor there is a chink or a weak human link in this chain. This had to be found! Luckily, we had Kees Koole and friends who spent time in these waters in their yacht and who gave us knowledgeable advice.

Another consideration in the planning was timing. When and under what conditions could we depart with the minimum of risk? It had to be on a moonless night at a high tide. Both of these required an up-to-date Nautical Almanac and the Manual of Tides. Both were prohibited articles to have in your possession unless by special permission from the German Navy. Even Tonnie could not safely get these. Fishing boats were only allowed outside with armed German soldiers, sailors or Dutch Nazi's on board. They handled these books. However, there was a way to get at this information. The skipper of the Lifeboat at Scheveningen harbor, Skipper de Bruyn, had them issued to him. This was a coincidence as I knew him very well, playing dominoes with him after Sunday church service at the upstairs flat of the church warden of the Oude

Scheveningsche Kerk. This was wheels-within-wheels as the church warden was a family connection of Bep van Oosten.

Skipper de Bruyn did not allow me to take his Almanac and Tide-tables. I had to see him in his small office in the harbor area where I copied the information we required. From these I drew two geometrical curves, one curve for the moon-phases, from (dark to full moon via its quarter phases or half-moons. The other curve was the predicted times and heights of high and low water for every day. These curves were drawn against a calendar/time grid. Where both curves met, one at dark moon and the other at high tide would be the best time for our move. The most favorable time would be after high tide when the tidewater would return to the sea, ebb-tide, and with an east wind which would work together to float the boat quietly out to sea. If that happened just after dark, indications showed us that we should leave on or about February 11, 1943.

A further requirement was to get a seaworthy motorboat; not an easy thing to accomplish. The word seaworthy was the fly in the ointment. All seaworthy vessels, such as seagoing fishing boats, were under lock and key, well-guarded in a harbor. We had to look at inland pleasure boats, which had to be strengthened to withstand high seas and needed to have stronger engines than what was required on lakes and waterways. These engines had to be rigged to withstand high humidity to prevent electrical breakdown. Tonnie purchased the Djemma, a seven-meter long motorboat from the Van Ravensteyn shipyard in Leidschendam. We were not aware at the time but learned later that Tonnie quietly organized a group of trustworthy chaps, unrelated to what we were doing and unaware that we existed. Their world of food supply and contact with the citizenry gathered useful information for our overseas Dutch government. He gathered this information in weighted waterproof envelopes for us to take to England.

We took care of other requirements like emergency kits, drinking water, and similar supplies. We planned for clothes we should wear but had no life jackets. They were not obtainable. Time was short, and we had to organize our crew.

Six Eager Beavers

It was early February 1943, and everything was set to go. The crew of six consisted of Anton (Tonnie) B. Schrader, the brothers Willy and Robert Weyhenke, Christiaan de Bakker, Johan A. Stroeve and Christiaan (Tip) Gutteling.

The Germans suppressed weather reports on the radio and in the papers, so we used the barometer, the wind compass and wind strength indicator in front of an optician's shop in The Hague. This optician also had a shop in Scheveningen where they posted a small notice in the window of conditions at sea for the benefit of holidaymakers at this sea resort. We watched these postings for a while to get a general picture of local weather conditions as a calm sea was important and fog a godsend.

Days before our departure, our group of six held a meeting at the flat of Mrs. Burgwall. She was Rudy Burgwall's mother and old friends of Tonnie. Tonnie instructed us on the following cover story for our personal security and safety and for those we left behind in case we fell into German hands and underwent Gestapo interrogation:

"We had met a small man who wore heavy black rimmed glasses. He offered to take us to England at a heavy price. We only saw him once. We had never met him before or since."

This was the gist of this story. But Tonnie tested us with a Gestapo-like interrogation and made us repeat a so-called Judas-word to use to warn others. He also told us to find a specific house in The Hague which was the house where we supposedly met at our departure. We were to memorize what the house looked like.

On the morning of the 11th we met near Smeelinck-plein after some of us took a quick look at the instruments in the optician's shop around the corner. Shortly afterwards we were picked up by a car which took us to Schipluiden. There Kees Koole stood ready with his forty-ton barge, the Nooit Volmaakt loaded with our small motorboat, the Djemma, covered with a canvas sheet and potatoes. There was a small space for us to hide under the canvas.

We felt the barge shudder when its engine started and sat waiting in the darkness of the hold, while Kees Koole took his barge from Schipluiden through the a canal to the Old Meuse, and then to the end of the Spui, a canal near a river outlet to the North Sea.

This was our departure spot before leaving The Netherlands. It was a lonely place and well tucked away on the side of a broad stretch of water. We did not have to wait long before the hatches were opened, and we could see the night sky. We were amazed at how much you could see when your eyes grew accustomed to the darkness.

We took our Djemma out of the hold of the barge using three heavy wooden poles, block-and-tackle, muscle power, and strong backs. We worked quietly and got our motorboat over the side, where, "Oh my God!" the motorboat slipped out of its tackle and fell into the water with a resounding smack. It broke a bottom

support beam, let in water and damaged the motor which refused to start. We held our breath as the noise could have been heard for miles around in the still of the night. But nothing stirred, and all remained quiet.

Kees Koole, the coolest and calmest of us all, put a tow rope across to the Djemme where we were bailing out bilge water. He towed the Djemma through the night all the way back to Schipluiden. He gave a friendly wave to the guard post who knew him as the government food-supplier. We all escaped with nothing worse than a bad recollection!

Postmortem

A review and analysis of our unsuccessful venture was now necessary for those who wished to try again. That was all of us, except Tonnie, who was asked to stay and assist other hopefuls.

We realized that our Djemma was too fragile and the engine was not satisfactory. Tonnie set about the task of organizing more escape boats. He selected and purchased these boats himself. They were found, with our assistance, and taken to the Van Ravensteijn shipyard in Schipluiden for a thorough check-up, strengthening and partial rebuild if necessary. The engines were checked and overhauled, made water-resistant or exchanged for a better suited engine. None of this could be done in Schipluiden. It had to be taken to an engineering workshop in Haaren, Noord Brabant; where the motor of our boat, a 2.8 liter, 26 hp Ford motor was overhauled and improved. These motorboats varied from seven to ten meters in length. All of this was expensive and the money for it had to be found. Some of the crew members were asked to contribute; for instance, Jaap Burger, a lawyer in the town of Dordrecht could well afford it. He paid twenty-five thousand guilders, half the price paid for our boat. Some wealthy friends and family of Tonnie donated the remainder. After the war, Tonnie declared that these finances were controlled by the National Relief Fund Foundation and that every contributor was repaid in full.

In early 1943, to control the movement of waterborne traffic and to suppress smuggling and the contraband trade in all the waterways of South-Holland and Zeeland, Tonnie created an official government service called the CCCD, or Central Crisis Control Service. All his motorboats had an official signboard stating in big letters: Control vessel. These vessels were under an official seal, which consisted of a simple cord with a lead seal. This made such an impression on the Germans that they returned one boat which tore itself loose and was drifting down river! It looked and was official. It was ready made for our motorboats, for now these boats did not need to be stowed into a barge. They could be legally towed by Kees Koole's barge into the Sperrgebiet or wherever. Only the eager beaver escapists had to be hidden in the barge. This was brilliant; the Germans understood officialdom and respected it.

The waterways to our departure point in the Haringvliet could be reached via three different locks, at Vlaardingen, Rotterdam, or Schiedam whose lock-gates were well guarded. So Kees Koole decided to alternate his use of them.

Jaap Burger, an avid yachtsman, who knew the Zeeland waterways and the North Sea, was in favor crossing to England in a sailing boat, but Tonnie persuaded him to be the skipper of the motorboat planned for early May 1943, which was our departure date.

For the second time, we stood ready to try again!

Eleven Feathers

On July 14, 1942, Karel A. de Munter, an electrical engineer, escaped from a prison in Scheveningen, known as Oranjehotel. He had been incarcerated on May 18, 1942, for an unsuccessful escape attempt from IJmuiden harbor in a fishing trawler with twelve others and which had German soldiers on board. Karel went into hiding in The Hague. My father put Karel in contact with Tonnie Schrader who agreed to have him on our boat as an extra crew member.

We got another extra crew member who was a radio operator, Mike Mora. He was from New Plymouth, New Zealand. Mike had parachuted out of a Short Sterling RAF bomber which was shot down by a German night fighter over Utrecht. Only Mike managed to evade the German search party. He was assisted by locals and went into hiding. Tonnie was contacted by Ben Reynders so now we had two more crewmembers, Mike and Ben.

"Truth is stranger than fiction," as the following narration will show! Gerard Bruyne, former chauffeur of Queen Wilhelmina, went with his boss, Tonnie Schrader, to pick up Mike Mora and take him to another hiding place near Schipluiden, our boarding point. They were stopped near the town of Woerden by two German military policemen on BMW motorbikes. Their official name was the Regular Police. Because of their dark green uniforms, they were called die Grünen.

They answered to the SS, and therefore to the Gestapo. They had a sub-branch that wiretapped telephones, traced secret radio-transmitters, and listened in on overseas radio stations. They were the motor-escort of their regional commander and told Tonnie that the commander's car had broken down. He requisitioned Tonnie's car to get him to his office in The Hague. The commander accepted Tonnie's invitation to travel with him, after Tonnie introduced himself as the Head of the Government Food Supply Office. He took his seat next to Tonnie in a backseat and off they went with a military escort in front of them. This was a bizarre set-up with an

RAF radio-operator and a German commander travelling in the same car. I never found out if Mike was scared but Tonnie was his usual self and kept the conversation going all the way to the commander's office, a few buildings away from Tonnie's office on the same street. They parted as great friends, inviting each other for a drink in their office. Luckily, this whole episode went off well with Mike Mora having a good story to tell.

Historical Note:

Mike Mora was killed over Germany on his next bombing trip.

The day before our departure we met again at Mrs. Burgwall's flat and were again treated to spicy fried rice. Tonnie Schrader gave us his lecture on security matters, after which we were set for tomorrow's departure.

The next morning, we met near the Sweelinckplein and some again studied the instruments at the optician's shop to get some idea of the weather awaiting us.

We were picked up by two cars which took us to Schipluiden where we boarded the Nooit Volmaakt barge. We hid ourselves in the hold under the potatoes, in a small compartment made up with a canvas; we just about fit if we squeezed tightly. We felt the shudder when the barge engine sprang to life and off we went down the canals and waterways with the barge towing our motorboat to the end of the Spui just past Goudzwaard. Our crew members were: Mr. Jaap A.W. Burger skipper, Christiaan de Bakker, Willy Weijhenke, Robert Weijhenke, Johan A. Stroeve, Piet H.de Groot, Cyril Michael (Mike) Mora, Gerard Bruyne, Ir. Karel A.de Munter, Bernard (Ben) Reynders and Christiaan (Tip) Gutteling. Kees Koole left us, as before, in the secluded small reed creek, wished us well, goodbye and good luck and returned to Schipluiden with his barge.

We waited for darkness and the start of ebb tide which was expected soon. We sat quietly as talking can be heard a long way off on the water. We whispered if anything had to be said and listened to the east wind and the cry of water birds. So far, so good!

Addendum: Tonnie Schrader and my sister, Willy, were waiting for the following radio message from the BBC Radio Nederland: "De adelaar heeft elf veertjes verloren." (The eagle has lost eleven feathers).

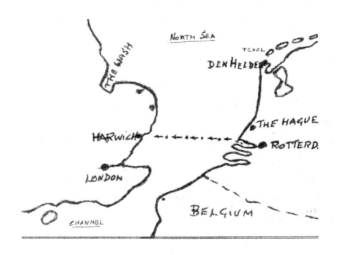

THIS MAP SHOWS THE DUTCH AND ENGLISH COASTS
BORDERING THE NORTH SEA . THE DOTTED LINE WAS
THE ROUTE WE TOOK (AS THE CROW FLIES)
DISTANCE : 110 nautical miles (approximately 180 km)

Seaborne

Our learned lawyer friend and skipper, Jaap Burger, told those of us who would be active during this voyage to be in readiness. For the rest were to keep quiet as the slightest noise could put us in danger.

Karel de Munter took his place near the engine and made things ready for a clean start when called for by the skipper. I placed myself by the compass, kneeling in front of it with my knees on sacking. I was ready to throw a cloth over my head and the compass as a blackout before switching on the compass dial light. This prevented any light from giving away our position.

At 22:45 dark with clouds, a breeze from the east, and the ebb tide building up its flow of water to the sea with everything near perfect for a change. The skipper stood by the steering wheel, gave the sign to let *go* of the rope holding us to the reeds and off we drifted. At first slowly and a bit rudderless but soon picking up speed drifting with the ebbtide. We were still at the end of the Spui turning to starboard into the broad waters of the Haringvliet, where a stronger ebb tide gave us more speed. We were now approximately seventeen km from the open sea and drifting nicely but not knowing how fast. After about an hour, we heard sand scraping the bottom of the boat. It wasn't long after that when we got stuck on a sandbank. With no time to lose, I jumped overboard and stood on the sand bank trying to push the boat back out to sea/ With the help of one other chap we managed to clear the boat and lead it by its bow to deeper water before jumping back in. It was a bit of a brrrrr, but I got warm soon with a blanket round me.

We were going fine again. And then we went aground again. This time without any warning from the sound of scraping sand. We were stuck fast for over an hour! We split into two teams, one pushing and the other pulling. We worked until we could hardly breathe. We had everyone out in the water to give the boat more buoyancy, but we were sitting ducks. We did not dare to start the noisy engine in fear of worse things happening. All of a sudden, by the kindness of the ebb tide, the boat, by its buoyancy, floated free again. What a relief! We were off again until someone whispered that there were two German guard ships or patrol boats vaguely visible in the dark on our left. They apparently had not yet noticed us. We kept very quiet, drifting forward until, out of the darkness on our left, we saw colored signal rockets going up with a loud swishhhh, which gave us a hell of a fright. The skipper tapped our engineer on the head. He started the engine with a roar and our boat responded immediately standing on its rear-end speeding forward with a capability of thirty-five km/hour.

I put the cloth over the compass and my head, switched on the compass dial-light, and waited for the skipper to tap my head for a compass reading. Needless to say, we did not reply to their signal to identify ourselves. There it came; pop, pop, pop, pop, and tracer bullets from heavy machineguns. The other crew members sat mesmerized and scared out of their wits as they told me later. They watched the tracer lights coming towards us and over us indicating that they could not see us too well.

We reckoned that the German boats must were about two to three hundred meters away from us in this dark night. They were stationed next to each other, so both could not open fire at the same time in case of hitting each other.

Fortunately, no one was hit but was the boat hit? We made a quick check for any water coming in, but as far as we could make out in the dark it seemed all right.

We were speeding away from Germans having taken them by surprise. It must have taken them some time to get up to speed and chase us. We felt the swell of the sea as we sped through the river mouth into the North Sea. The coastal defense response came a bit later. We could see colored signal rockets going up all along the coast. Although we could not see the coast, these rockets showed us the approximate coast line. Then suddenly, searchlights came, going straight up into the sky, then slowly down to sea level coming towards us from different coastal positions. They tried to put us into a cross-light. Then the boom of heavy guns and waterspouts around us where their shells hit the water. But by now we were well away on the sea in the darkness. The waves made us bob up and down and with our low profile we were very difficult to spot. Then we heard the scream of a shell flying low over us, hitting the sea not far from us. It threw up an awful lot of water which hit us hard and shook the boat. We made a quick check to see if we were all still on board and were washed overboard. Luckily all were present but shaken. The engineer reported water coming in from the bow so we made a big ball from sacking, blankets, and clothing, and wedged it into the bow space.

To keep this big cloth plug in place and hard against the big crack, one of us had to lie on his back on a bed of clothing and hold the plug in place by pressing it with his feet. We took turns on this job as the cramped space made it tiring. This must have been a lucky shot as the shooting stopped all together and all was quiet again; except for the retching sound of some poor chaps who became seasick or from nervous tension. It was now 02:00. in the morning and the skipper had taken our boat to bear west to correct for the change of tides. The straight-line distance from the Hoek of Holland to Harwich is one hundred and ten nautical miles.

At 03:00, a crew member appointed as lookout to watch the rear reported four fast moving boats right behind us about a mile away. They could be (Motor Torpedo Boats sent out to find and destroy us). The skipper threw our boat into a sharp turn to starboard heading due north to get the hell out of their way. At this early hour, a haze hung over the sea and with our low profile we could probably get away. We did, as they turned south and disappeared over the horizon. This again shows that one always needs a little bit of luck!

After ten minutes, we went due west again and at about 11:00 we passed some sea mines and two corpses floating on their lifejacket. Then we noticed some low flying bombers flying to the west and we waved to them.

At about 12:00 we saw smoke on the western horizon, then some balloons, then a convoy of ships, which we approached slowly until an English warship, a sloop or a frigate, came towards us. In order not to become a sitting duck to possible enemy submarines or aircraft, they never stopped. They turned to get us on their lee side so we could get on board in a calmer sea. We were thrown a rope. At low speed we came alongside and clambered up a rope ladder and got on board.

As the last man left our motorboat, the English sailors tried to winch her on board, but she took on water quickly and sank. She had done her duty to the last and we stood there feeling a great loss! It was 01:30 and we were elated, feeling so relieved as tons of pent-up tension and strain fell away from us! English officers and men were very kind, feeding us, giving us sailors clothes, as most of us had nothing on but our underpants.

Addendum: The details of this escape are given in the official report No: 2847 of the Nederlandse Veiligheids Dienst (Netherlands Secret Service).

abridged translation of the overleaf document (page 7⁵)

This is a copy of **Report No.2847** - from: Chief of Police - Outside Services - and addressed to: Minister of Justice -   with reference to: case No.10. Gutteling, Christiaan.

This report gives an abridged version of my escape report given at my interrogation, and as given in full on pages 71 to 75; from organising it to carrying it out, until I landed at Harwich on the 6th May 1943 at 4.30 hr pm.

At the bottom, between brackets, is the following statement : -
(To be considered for a decoration.)

PART 5—FREEDOM

The final emergence into freedom, only those who have experienced it can appreciate it.

Patriotic School

The Royal Victoria Patriotic School (RVPS) was situated in London at Clapham in the Borough of Wandsworth. Originally built in 1857, its foundation stone was laid by Queen Victoria/ It was called the Royal Victoria Patriotic Asylum for the orphan daughters of soldiers and sailors killed in the Crimean War.

In 1939, at the beginning of World War II, the girls were evacuated to make way for a detention and interrogation centre with prison cells and it became the home of MI5 and MI6 for the primary purpose of catching enemy spies. We simply called it the Patriotic School.

After the war, this building was renovated into twenty-nine luxury apartments, twenty-five studios, workshops, and a drama school. It was renamed the Royal Victoria Patriotic Building with a restaurant holding a license to register marriages called La Gothique.

This was an introduction to our home-away-from-home for the following two weeks as guests of the British Secret Service. It was going to be interesting to observe the difference between their methods and those of the Gestapo, as their terms of reference must have been nearly identical.

On May 6, 1943, I landed blindfolded on British soil, more precisely on the quayside of Harwich harbor, guided by a sailor. He took me into a building where they allowed me to take off my blindfold.

I was requested to undress and was thoroughly examined by a doctor. After that I took a bath, which smelled of carbolic acid antiseptic, under the watchful gaze of a male attendant. I then had a cup of coffee and a piece of cake and slept in an easy chair. I was awakened by two civilians in dark blue coats and hats. They introduced themselves as being from the police and had come to take me to London asking me to please put my clothes on. All I had was what I had on, a pair of sailors' trousers and a navy-blue jersey which was given to me on board the British Navy Sloop. (My underpants were taken away which made the trousers very itchy.) One of the policemen left the room and came back a little later with underpants, a pair of socks, shoes and a navy-blue raincoat. After changing into my new clothes, we were off.

We went to a nearby harbor railway siding where a train, with old fashioned coaches, stood waiting. We boarded a reserved compartment. The windows were covered with a light green cloth preventing me from looking out. Each policeman took a seat next to one of the doors with me sitting in the middle of the seats opposite them. All this time, little was spoken, as the English language did not come easy to me although I had English at school. Language fluency and the quick understanding of what was said was a different matter. It made for halting conversation and often created misunderstanding. They were kind, patient and spoke slowly. They gave me a cigarette to smoke, but tiredness and the clickety-click rhythm of the wheels put me fast asleep! All this time I had not seen any of the other crew members.

We arrived at a station and I was told that we had reached London. I was led to a police car, which also had covered windows.

Eventually, we arrived at a large Victorian looking multi-storied building where I was handed over to a receptionist in army uniform. He took the papers from my police escort, wished me luck and left.

The receptionist looked up from reading these papers and smilingly asked me to follow her. She opened a door and led me into a small bedroom where she left me locking the door behind her.

It was all so strange, different, and new. I sat down on the bed, put my head in my hands and tried to take it all in! It wasn't long until there was a knock at the door and a British army officer came in. In fluent Dutch he wished me good day, asked if I was all right and requested that I follow him. He took me to an office, where we sat opposite each other across a desk. After checking my credentials, he asked if I needed any sort of medical care. I did not. He told me what building I was in; that it was well guarded but that I could freely walk around its corridors and garden area unless a display or signboard said otherwise. He said that all interrogation would be carried out in Dutch. Otherwise, English would be spoken by everyone. I would soon be contacted by a housekeeper who would show me the toilets and bathrooms, the dining room, and other areas. He asked if I had any personal needs. I did not. He told me that we were on the first floor and gave me my room number. We shook hands, he told me I was free to move around in the building, held open the door for me to leave and wished me well.

That was the end of the official proceedings on my first day in Britain.

Trustworthy

At the beginning of World War II, the British Secret Service was overwhelmed by the detailed work it had to handle. It quickly had created other departments or enlarged existing ones, such as:

MI5. Military Intelligence Department Five already existed. It was the counter espionage and security services but was enlarged to investigate the trustworthiness of all persons entering Britain coming from enemy territory. (Trust-worthiness basically meant having a mind-set to be for the Allies an against the Axis forces.)

MI6. Military Intelligence Department Six was created to become the British Secret Intelligence Service (SIS). It was mainly interested in getting information on escape routes for downed British air-crews.

MI9. Military Intelligence Department Nine was established to create and set-up escape routes for downed British aircrews based on the information passed to it by MI6.

SOE: Special Operations Executive was in charge of sabotage and subversion in enemy territory and sending out agents or teams for this purpose.

The forgoing is a basic introduction to the purpose for which the Royal Victoria Patriotic School (RVPS) was taken over by Military Intelligence. We were engaged by all these services in turn, starting with MI5 to establish our trustworthiness. At that time, we were not aware of these facts and went through the mill sheepishly, being questioned by various persons.

Life in detention in the Royal Patriotic School was not unpleasant. The food and drinks were satisfactory; the sleeping arrangements were good; there were newspapers and reading matter in many languages, including Dutch; the bath-tubs were too small as they were made for children, but they were sufficient for a wash; all-in-all not bad! There was a big garden which looked out on to railway tracks where I watched trains speeding by. Otherwise, we were contained within the premises without any contact with the outside world.

The interrogation sessions were friendly, professional, firm and tenacious. They wanted to get to the bottom of things by finding out if the narrator was consistent with the truth or was a clever storyteller. Their cross examination could take hours if the interrogator was not fully satisfied with the answers. The intensity of the cross examination determined the duration of your stay at the Royal Patriotic School, which could be a week or more.

In my case, it was over in about three or four days. There was a change of interrogators who asked more mundane questions about your observations in enemy territory, such as: the German army and navy signs on cars, lorries, vessels, and other vehicles which would indicate to them what units they belonged to or were there signs they did not know about. They also asked about the different types of radio or radar aerials you saw; types of ships of war, armored cars and tanks, and other equipment, for which they had many books, full of drawings and pictures of different types of equipment, such as the aircraft-recognition book.

When the time came that I was declared to be politically reliable and trustworthy, I was transported to the Netherlands Secret Service. To be more precise, a section of it known as the Politie-Buitndienst (PBD) or Police Foreign Service. They worked closely with MI5. I thought this was duplication after the British had declared me trustworthy!

I met Colonel Oresto Pinto (1889–1961) from the Politie Buitendienst, a sharp, intelligent, older Dutch officer. He was reputed as being a clever spy catcher since his younger days in World War I when the British Secret Service made good use of this multi-language speaking Dutchman although The Netherlands were not at war. He was forthright to the point of being rude and tried to scare me and confuse me and put me on the offensive. But I kept my cool as I had nothing to hide or feel guilty about. Eventually he shook hands with me and told me that I was in the clear.

He wrote the final report about me. On the bottom he wrote that he recommended me for a decoration. (Report No. 2847 van Chef Politie Buitendienst aan de Minister van Justitie.) I was now free!

Cadet in training at the 63rd Naval Observer Course - Oct'43 to May'44 in Scotland

Epilogue

This epilogue deals with the so called loose ends that round off my narration. First, there were Engelandvaarders or England-farers. They are Dutch people who are best known to themselves. They took great risks during World War II to get to England. (On the Continent of Europe, we use the United Kingdom or Britain.) There were three routes:

Route One; The North Sea route.
Route Two; The Southern route via Switzerland, Spain
    and Portugal.
Route Three; The Scandinavian route.

In total seventeen hundred and six persons tried to escape from the Netherlands and only ten percent made it. This is as far as is known. Some may have perished in trying.

Route One via the North Sea was the shortest, but the most difficult to organize and the most dangerous. Those fleeing had to go through the heavily armed coastal strip known as the Atlantic Wall. One hundred and thirty-six attempts were made. Only thirty-one were successful. Out of the overall total of 1706 persons, 172, or 10 percent, made it via Route One.

Route Two, the Southern route via Switzerland, Spain and Portugal, took an average of fifteen months to reach Britain. People had to deal with long and tiring distances and the risks of being imprisoned in those countries. Some even settled there. Of the overall total of 1706, 985 or 50 percent made it.

Route Three, the Scandinavian route was difficult to assess. This route was only available to sailors or stowaways. Many liked Scandinavia so much that they settled there quietly.

As the Engelandvaarders were few, their military contribution was small. Those who became secret-agents and went back by parachute or boat, played a substantial role, although many were killed by the Germans.

Anton Bernard Schrader, or Tonnie to us, organized or assisted eight escape-boats with sixty-four persons. Only two boats with twenty-three persons, or 36 percent, arrived in Britain. One person, T.J. Vrins, tried it three times and never made it. Two persons, A.B. Schrader and C. Gutteling, tried it twice and made it on the second attempt. Tonnie Schrader's successful escape to Britain took place on October 8, 1943, in the last boat he organized together with eleven crew-members.

On his arrival in England, Tonnie was not trusted by the British or Dutch Secret Services. After two or three weeks, he was given the benefit of the doubt and released. This made it nearly impossible for him to find suitable employment. Tonnie then turned to the American OSS (Office of Strategic Services), the predecessor of the CIA (Central Intelligence Agency), and was accepted. He was trained and in November 1944, dropped as agent Bobby over Ulrum in Groningen in the Netherlands. It is noteworthy that this dropping was against the wish of the Netherlands authorities.

In February 1945, Schrader was arrested by the German SD who used his radio operator's skills to make a radio-play, as the Germans called it, against the Americans in London. Schrader, however, used his Judas procedure, by using the word damn as often as he could, without arousing suspicion. It worked. The Americans now knew that he was under the control and pressure of the Germans.

While being interrogated, Tonnie gave the strong impression that the Allies were planning an invasion in the Deutsche Bucht with Bremerhaven as its centre point. The Germans took this information very seriously and acted by sending two tank divisions from the Rhine area to the Bremen area in North Germany. After the war, General Eisenhower told Tonnie that in captivity he had done more good than he realized as the American forces were able to cross the Rhine with considerably fewer losses against the depleted German armor.

American President Harry S. Truman conferred the Silver Star Medal; on Tonnie. It is the highest honor the USA awards non-

Americans. Only two were awarded in World War II. The Dutch authorities changed their minds and gave Tonnie the Bronze Cross, the same as I received from Queen Wilhelmina.

I.B.23

The Bearer *Christiaan GUTTELING* who

states that he is of *Dutch*

nationality, is permitted to land at

on condition that

PERMITTED TO LAND AT LONDON ON CONDITION THAT THE HOLDER JOINS THE *Dutch* ... ARMED FORCES IN ACCORDANCE WITH ARRANGEMENTS ... BE BY THE *Dutch Consul* IN LONDON AND ... SUBJECT CON- DITIONS AS ... THE HOLDER IS DISCHARGED ... IN THE UNITED ...

(Signed) *W. M. ...*

Immigration Officer's Stamp.

IMMIGRATION OFFICER
(2)
24 MAY 1943
LONDON

Signature of Bearer

Have you ever heard of a Ministry of Authority? Of course not, because authority is the generic term for a whole group or category of people who have some power or right to enforce obedience or give an ultimate decision.

Following is a summary of such a gaggle of people. We may as well have come from outer space when we were picked up by one of the British Authorities; the Royal British Navy. We were handed over to the police, one of the fifty-two police forces in Britain, who quickly transported us to the British Secret Service who, after finding that I was trustworthy, handed me over to the Netherlands Secret Service. They duplicated matters and found me to be politically trustworthy and handed me over to the Royal Netherlands Consulate. Their duty was to get me through the Immigration Office in London and get a Certificate IB23 stating that I was permitted to land at London on condition that I join the Dutch armed forces. This Certificate was obtained May 24, 1943. Now, the Dutch Consulate had to get me off their hands and into the armed forces, who would then be responsible for me for the rest of the war!

Wow, there I was, in London in May 1943 having just joined the Royal Netherlands Navy to be trained to become a navigator in the Fleet Air Arm. I was excited and keen to make a start on Wale Island in Portsmouth; Pomey to sailors. Apart from having to do everything at the double; for example; running, square bashing or drilling, we learned all about the fall of shot of naval guns and how to observe and report from the air and judge the type of waterspout their gunfire would throw up. We also learned to key Morse code messages under the stands of the Lords Cricket Field while housed in a hotel in London. From Queen Wilhelmina I received an audience at her country estate near Maidenhead. I got the Bronze Cross, equivalent to the British George Cross for civilians, equivalent to the Silver Cross in the United States, or the Distinguished Service Order for Officers of all Arms; on July 29, 1943.

PROUD AS A PEACOCK (TROTS ALS EEN PAUW)
1st June 1947
Just commissioned as Sub-Lieutenant Observer RNR in the Royal Netherlands
Fleet Air Arm wearing my newly acquired Observers Wings.
(Net benoemd tot Luitenant ter zee Waarnemer der derde klasse KMR in de
Koninklijke Marine Luchtvaart Dienst met mijn nieuwe Waarnemers-vleugels)

What follows is a narrative of what happened to me after I had arrived on British territory, safe and sound, on May 5, 1943, from German occupied Holland.

I tried to be as precise as possible; not pedantic or in the style of a novel but as it happened. My memory at times, had to rely on old documents, logbooks and photographs. Some were discolored or become faint, but they were helpful in showing the present reader what a different world we lived in. I dedicate this to fallen Comrades.

DAWN PATROL

RETURNING TO BASE FROM A SEARCH FOR STRAGGLERS

AFTER A GERMAN U-BOAT NIGHT ATTACK ON THE CONVOY

Hr.Ms."Karel Doorman" in Cape Town harbour

8 January 1947

Ltz.Waarnemer 2e.klasse OC - C.Gutteling BK·
Signals Officer (Verbindings-Officier) on the
Escort Carrier Hr.Ms."Karel Doorman",

(ex HMS."Nairana"- white-eagle in Maori)

In the gracious presence of Her Majesty The Queen

The Prime Minister and Her Majesty's Government
in the United Kingdom of Great Britain and Northern Ireland
extend an invitation to

Mr C. Gutteling

to attend a
Service of Thanksgiving, Reconciliation and Hope
to commemorate the 50th Anniversary of
The End of War in Europe
in St Paul's Cathedral on Sunday 7th May 1995 at 11 am

R.S.V.P. by 31st March 1995
VE/VJ Day
PO Box 1940, Fairford
Gloucestershire GL7 4NA
Telephone: 0171-824 2845

Dress: See Reverse
Guests should be seated by 10 am

By Kind Permission of the Dean and Chapter of St Paul's Cathedral

Tickets will be sent to those accepting
(This invitation will not allow admittance to St Paul's)

PART 6—BEGINNING

Perfection is based on well laid fundamentals.

At the Beginning

The unexpected and the unforeseen happen to you when you arrive from German enemy territory in an England at war.

I had never seen an English sailor, soldier or air-man in uniform or, for that matter, an English person. I spoke bookish or pedantic English, learned at school and college where we were also taught the English diphthongs which are so strikingly different from ours in The Netherlands.

For instance, the "th" in the word "the" would be pronounced by us as "de"; thus, the English word thirty would come out as dirty (The answer to a question could become: "I am dirty, and my brother is dirty too." How embarrassing!) Much time was devoted to learning the correct pronunciation of the English language. There were many pitfalls, but in the end, we acquired the gist of it and repeated and sang American songs which we picked up from radio broadcasts.

Having been cleared and declared trustworthy by the Secret Services, permitted to land by the Immigration Office, handed over to my compatriots, and I was compelled to join the Armed Forces. I had to choose which service I wished to join. I chose to learn how to fly and to become a fighter pilot.

My request to be trained as a pilot was refused. Pilots had a short training period and it takes a much longer period to teach the intricacies of the art of navigation and observation. When you are already a fully qualified navigator for the Merchant Navy you are eminently suitable to join the Fleet Air Arm. That was that. I was conscripted and enrolled into the Netherlands Royal Navy on May 30, 1943, with the rank of Leading Seaman. I counted myself lucky at not having been drafted into the Merchant Navy, but I still did not know what was in store for me.

My first duty was to report to the Netherlands Naval Store and be supplied with my new Leading Seaman's uniform with all the other items normally issued; underwear, socks, shoes, duffle-coat, and the rest. All this gear needed a large kit-bag as sailors were expected to carry all their possessions themselves. A car from the Royal Netherlands Navy was waited to take me to the store. The sailor driver looked at me as if I had just crawled out an apple. He asked me where my luggage was. I told him I had none, and he indicated to follow him. I must have looked peculiar to him in my bits and pieces of clothing given to me by various kind persons. We soon became friendly on our way through London after I had told him that I had recently escaped from The Netherlands; that opened a floodgate of questions!

We soon arrived at the naval store where I was introduced to the officer in charge of stores. He took my papers and told an NCO (Non-Commissioned Officer) to provide me with the necessary full outfit for a Leading Seaman.

My driver said he would wait for me and sat down on a chair opening a newspaper. The NCO told me to follow him into the store, and I said, "Yes, sir."

He turned round saying loudly in a commanding voice, "Do not call me Sir, call me Major, which is the manner one addressed a petty officer in my Navy. My learning curve had started! When the right size in everything I needed was finished and it was neatly laid out on a trestle-table, I had to check off item by item on a pre-printed list and sign. I was told, in no uncertain tones, to get undressed and put on one set of my underwear. My driver helped me dress in my uniform, putting it on in the right order and in the right way. He showed me how to stow the rest in my new kit-bag. Everything went in, except my duffle coat, overcoat and raincoat. I was Leading Seaman from the cap down!

"Teach him to salute every uniform that does not look like his," said the NCO. "Take care; don't make a fool of yourself!"

He also said, "Take him to his digs. His movement orders and travel warrant are waiting for him. Tomorrow morning he'll have to move to Portsmouth where his training will start at Whale Island." (No rest for the wicked.)

"Off we go now to Oranje Haven where you are booked for the night," said the driver cheerfully. "It is a house that Queen Wilhelmina has bought for the use of Engelandvaarders, like yourself. It is a club and has some bedrooms, so you should feel very honored." Oranje Haven is a big house at 23 Hyde Park Place not far from Marble Arch.

We arrived in the late afternoon on a lovely summer's day and were cordially received with a welcome cup of tea and cake and an apple. I said good-bye and thanked my driver. I was shown to my small but neat bedroom where an official looking letter awaited my attention. I opened and studied it with great care and found some paper money and coins of different values. There was a railway travel warrant to take me from Waterloo Station to Portsmouth, where a British Royal Navy lorry marked Whale Island or Gunnery School or both would take me to my destiny.

I also found my Pay Book which also acted as my identity document with my number 90544z. A small handwritten note informed me that a Navy car would pick me up at 08:00 to take me to Waterloo Station and see me onto the right train.

Wow, they got me taped!

I sat on the bed with all these papers and money around me and I lay back and looked at the ceiling to take all this in and wondered what had happened to me and fell into a deep sleep.

HMS Raven—Whale Island

Portsmouth and Gosport towns are in the County of Hampshire. These two towns straddle Portsmouth Harbor. They are traditional Royal Naval harbor towns with various affiliated services and training facilities.

Whale Island is situated on the east side of the Harbor and is part of Portsmouth; Pompey in the sailor's jargon. But it is an island surrounded by water. The Harbor waters lap its south, west, and north sides and a canal on its east side which has a bridge connecting it to Portsmouth. When World War II started in earnest, the small naval establishment at Dover had to evacuate to Whale Island when Dover came under the bombardment of the large German guns across the Channel in France. In my time, Whale Island or HMS Raven was a well- established place with old buildings surrounding a huge parade ground where newcomers into the Navy were taught the finer points of parading, the choreography of military marching in procession for the purpose of the disciplined movement of forces or for great ostentatious display. This training was vulgarly known as Square Bashing.

On June 1, 1943, I arrived at Whale Island in a Royal Navy lorry which had picked me up at the railway station. The lorry driver had picked up many Royal Navy Sailors.

At the ancient stone bridge that lead to the entrance of Whale Island we went through an archway where we stopped at a security bar. An armed sentry lifted the bar and let us through to the guard house.

We were ushered into the stone guardhouse where, to my surprise, I met two other Dutch Leading Seaman. In Dutch we made a quick mutual introduction. It must have sounded like Double Dutch to all the other sailors! After a while, we were lined up in a queue and were told to pipe down. We looked at each other, as we did not understand. I asked the sailor in front of us what it meant, and he answered, "It means shut up and be quiet."

134

The loud voice said, "Pay attention, this is a roll call," and started calling out names.

Sailors would answer yes or aye.

When the list was complete, the voice said, "Fall in outside the Guard House and await further orders." All the sailors shuffled outside.

That left the three of us Dutch Sailors standing. The voice coming towards us said, "Our gallant Allies, welcome to Whale Island." He was a pleasant looking chief petty officer who said, "We have all your details supplied to us from your Headquarters; you must be Aden, Van Tin, and Gutteling. All this may be a bit strange to you but do your best and you'll get through. Join the chaps outside and you'll be marched to your quarters where you'll find your kitbag on your bunk. Good luck."

We were marched off under the orders of a petty officer to a building with alphabetic markings A to C above the door. After we were dismissed, we were told to go to the first floor where Company B had its quarters. Here we found our kitbags; mine was on bunk number eleven in a row of fifteen bunks on the west side facing a row of fifteen bunks on the east side. The three Dutch Sailor's bunks were next to each other. Most of us sat on our bunk but not for long. The same petty officer came in and told us to unpack and stow our goods and chattels into our metal locker. Tomorrow we would be instructed in how to make up a bunk and how to stow our kit into our locker the Royal Navy way as no other way would be tolerated!

Our general orders were piped through the public-address system. "Be ready by 18:00 hours to go to your mess for your evening meal. Carry on." That gave us a fore-taste of the strict disciplinary manner with which we would be treated from now on.

We were detailed to be Squad B for the purpose of parading exercises. The whole establishment was divided into squads of thirty men each. We had to march three abreast with the tallest in front and the shortest member of the squad in the rear. We had to do the intricate parade movements in a military manner, over and over again until we could do it in our dreams.

We received lectures on naval and military matters; we learned to salute officers only as a mark of respect and to honor their Royal Commission.

You did not salute the man but the uniform which reflected the rank of his Commission. You only salute if both are in full uniform which includes head-gear. It is of interest to note that United States forces also salute each other hatless. You had to stand at attention when being spoken to or when speaking to an officer which is the military attitude of showing respectful attentiveness.

When in uniform, you represent the Royal Navy and have to dress correctly and be of implacable behavior, bearing, and manners. They threw the whole naval and military do's and don'ts at us until almost no individuality was left. We had just about become parading, marching, "Yes Siring," "No Siring," saluting, and running on-the-double robots covered in spit and polish.

There was a full parade on Sundays all who worked or underwent training in Whale Island with all the Squads assembled in a large rectangle around the parade ground for inspection by the Commander of Whale Island. This was followed by a display of marching past his dais, where he took the salute while the Royal Naval band played their best. At the end of this first Sunday Parade, the Parade Master gave the loud command, "Roman Catholics fallout," we wondered why this was done.

We saw many Sailors, out of the corner of our eyes, make an about-turn and walk away from the parade ground. After this interlude, we were all marched into a church which was set for an official church service with an altar. A priest stood in his gown and bands round his neck as if he was a Roman Catholic priest. After this service and a religious sermon, we queried. We were told that we had experienced a Church of England service in the military style. All non Church of England persons would be excused from attending. We could register at the Guard House as Church of Holland. We did this and at every Sunday Parade since then we fell-out, walked off the Parade Ground, and had extra time for ourselves. (There was no such church in The Netherlands, but nobody seemed to care.) The character of our additional stay in Whale Island became repetitious. One fine day we received the order to report to the Guard House.

What was up? We were relieved to receive the orders from our London Headquarters to return to London in two days' time. We would get our Travel Warrants and transport to and from the railway station.

We had been in Whale Island for approximately twenty-three days.

Dots and Dashes

Utterly unbelievable. Each of us was quartered in his own small room on the top floor of the Cumberland Hotel. We were roughly opposite Marble Arch facing south and Oxford Road and right on the doorstep of the wartime nightlife area of entertainment. This area was made up of that part of London contained within the corner markers of Marble Arch, Hyde Park Corner, Piccadilly Circus, and Oxford Circus. We were still very uninformed about all this, but we quickly caught on to where to find various night clubs such as the Coconut Grove, the Cuba Cabana, the Wing Club, the Allied Club, the French, Netherlands and American Clubs, and various pubs, restaurants, and so on. All that limited us was our meager pay packets, but the cosmopolitan society of wartime London was very generous to servicemen. Many clubs were open to all Allied Forces. We still had to be alert as the Military Police of all Allied Forces were everywhere, to keep peace and dampen any raucous and disgraceful behavior!

What we valued most and what suited our financial condition was an eating establishment called Lyons Corner House next door to the Cumberland Hotel. Its buffet style help-yourself system, its choice of lovely salads and helpful waitresses who people called Nippys. So much for the fun. What about our training matters? Of all places, we had to report to Lord's Cricket Ground at 08:00 on July 1, 1943. We were not to get lessons on how to play cricket but to learn to communicate in Morse Code; the dots and dashes language of radio communication at that time.

We still did things in the Whale Island disciplinary mode. In the early morning of July first, we took a bus ride from Marble Arch, along Edgeware Road and St. John's Wood Road and arrived at Lord's Cricket Ground far too early. The Royal Air Force guard at the gate enquired sarcastically if we were an Early dawn Dutch raiding party. We assured him that he was quite safe and had nothing to fear. He called his mate in the guard hut shouting, "Friendly Dutchies, please show them round."

138

So, we said in repartee, "Thank you Limey."

After all this geniality, the other guard showed us where we had to report at 08:00 then took us to their canteen where a Navy, Army, and Air Force Institutes canteen service girl served us a welcome cup of coffee.

Exactly at 0800 we registered in an office under the main grandstand! We found that this training establishment was run under the auspices of the RAF but, they made use of instructors from nearly every part of the British Forces and even from Merchant Navy radio operators. We were in a training group of twelve Royal Naval personnel of our rank of Leading Seamen. Mutual introductions were soon made in an easy, friendly and casual manner.

The instructors left us alone for a while to allow us to get acquainted. We learned that this whole group was destined to become Fleet Air Arm Observers if we made it through the training. There were two Observer Training Centers, one on the island of Trinidad, West Indies and the other near Arbroath, Angus, Scotland. Wow, that was food for thought!

An RAF flight lieutenant came into the room and we all stood up to attention. He introduced himself, told us to stand at ease and said, "This is not Whale Island, but, it is also not a holiday camp, as you will soon realize. Concentrated effort is required of you to master the art of communication by Morse Key. We all hope that you make it and I am sure that you will not let us down. It is nearly coffee time. I wish you all the strength you need to see you through."

As he walked out of the room, the Tannoy clicked on and declared that it was coffee break.

After thirty minutes of coffee-break, the Tannoy declared that all hands had to return to their station. Coming back to our room we met our class instructor. He was a petty officer of the Royal Navy who had the radio operators badge, the Americans called him a telegraphist and the British good naturedly called him Sparks. He introduced himself and told us that this was not our training room, and would we please follow him.

As a point of interest; we lived at a time when communication, or as the Navy called it signals, consisted of hoisted flag signals; semaphore with handheld flags; light signals using the Aldislamp and for longer distances, the searchlight and wireless telegraphy. In its early technological stage, it used the Morse Code to express alphabetic letters and numerical figures. Radiotelephony was still in its development stage although the American Air Force used the early Radio Telephony equipment with crystal controlled higher frequencies.

We entered a room, furnished with three rows of five separate small tables and chairs each. One large table at the front of this room faced the fifteen smaller tables. A blackboard was directly behind the big table. A typical ordinary classroom, one would say, except that every table had a Morsekey, a set of headphones, a couple of mounted switches, and an instrument that had a coil of white paper tape wound on a reel, and a big glass ashtray. The main table had all that plus all sorts of other gadgets and instruments. Furthermore, there were fifteen metal lockers and one large metal cupboard. The room had a full set of windows on one side and was nice and light. Our instructor invited us to choose any table except the three tables at the back. Each table had a double-digit number; 01, 02, 03, to 14 and 15. The fifteen lockers matched the tables.

When we were all seated our instructor said, "This will be your home-from-home for the duration of your stay, which will be approximately three months. No eating or drinking is allowed in this room. Please keep it clean, especially those that smoke. There are waste-paper baskets at the back for this purpose. Keep your lockers locked at all times. The last one who leaves this room must check that all power is switched off and then switch off the lights. You'll soon get the hang of it."

"We will now start with your training on how to communicate with each other, at a great distance using specialized equipment. Like speaking and writing, your message has only come across when you know that the other party has correctly received it by an acknowledgement. If your writing is bad or your speech is garbled, reception and understanding are impossible. So it is with radio communication. If you are quicker or better than your recipient, adopt the speed that makes it possible for him to receive and understand you. The key word is always Reception; make sure you have transmitted your message correctly and get confirmation of its reception. Conversely, do not give a confirmation until you have the whole message. All very logical and natural, until you meet up with the reality of bad atmospherically disturbances."

"You have in front of you on your table a Morse key which has a piece of thick felt under it to deaden the clicking noise of fifteen keys once you all start going in this room. This is normally not provided. This is a heavy brass key as used on our ships and shore stations. The key in our planes are much lighter and smaller. Your key is not fixed to your table, so you can use it right as well as left handed. Take a good look at it. You'll see that the contact gap can be adjusted to your liking. Don't make it too large as it will reduce your speed. Try it and see if you can key dots and dashes." He left us alone for a while to clatter away to our heart's content. Not long after, the Tannoy declared that it was lunch time. "Don't forget to put on your hats," said our instructor.

It did not take us long to find our canteen. After one hour's lunch break, in which we had a quick look at the cricket ground, we were all back in our classroom again, clattering away on our Morse keys, until our instructor knocked on his table, like a chairman with his gavel demanding attention.

"Each of you will find on his table a card printed with the Morse alphabet a list of Morse-numerals. Rhythm is very important in keying your Morse. Get used to this. We will start with the numerals, which have a mixture of five dots The War and dashes. Look at the list; notice that they have a logical numerical sequence, such as one has one dot and four dashes, two has two dots and three dashes, and so on up to five which has five dots. Six has one dash and four dots, seven has two dashes and three dots, and son up to nine with four dashes and one dot, followed by Zero which has five dashes. Try to key these out in their sequence, over and over again until you get the feel of some rhythm. Do not go too fast, the rhythm is the important thing. Off you go!"

So the classroom was filled with our clattering Morsekeys. After keying all the numerals for a while, we were called to attention, told to plug in our headphones and to do the same thing while listening to our own transmission and try to get a better rhythm. This was the first time that we heard the radio signals of our own. It sounded uneven and wavering. So we kept at it until our signal settled down to something like a steady rhythm, while at the same time we kept the numerals separate, instead of producing a stream of dots and dashes.

We were so steeped in our work that most of us did not hear the Tannoy declaring the end of our first working day, until our instructor switched-off all of our equipment and said, "See you tomorrow morning at 08:00 sharp."

Interpolation

Learning a new language, especially one without human vocal sounds, but one with a chirpy sound in coded form is difficult! You have to learn and remember a whole new set of alphabetic and numeral characters until it becomes second nature to you.

You do not have time to think. Listening and instant understanding is the norm to speaking and understanding any new language, so it is with the Morse code at high speed. What follows in this chapter is a description of this tedious method of training which can be very boring to read. If you want to take it for granted that we were well trained and passed this training course, you can skip the rest of this chapter.

Morse Coding

The next morning saw most of us in the canteen with a cup of tea well before time. At 08:00 sharp, we were all at our table, as our instructor walked in with a, "Good morning all. Yesterday was a bit of an introduction. Today, I would like to emphasize most strongly that you must know your Morse alphabet by heart, back-to-front and any other way. You must know it so well, that it becomes part of you! The sooner, the better! The Morse speed used at sea, by all shipping, is very fast and telegraphist can belt out and understand speeds of up to twenty-eight words per minute. We will try and get you up to twenty words per minute, or roughly one hundred letters per minute, or one point sixty-six letters per second. That is your task ahead of you! "With your alphabetic list next to you, key all the letters from A to Z with your head phones on, as you did yesterday with the numerals."

We did that until coffee break.

Coming back into our training room, the mysterious paper-tape unit fixed to our table was explained. It was a message recorder on which an ink pen would record each Morse character, giving an exact dots and dashes copy of our keying showing exactly what we did wrong or right. Each of us was also handed a strip of cardboard with half a page of typewritten text on it, which we had to transmit in Morse Code with the aid of our alpha list.

"Do not hurry; there is no race to be won. It is more important that you do it right, with the right spacing. Make sure that your Morse characters do not look like one string of dots and dashes and that your words do not run into each other, giving them a larger space between words than between characters or letters. Give it a try. I shall listen to each of you from my table, and we shall discuss your mistakes in detail afterwards."

We worked until tea break until the Tannoy squawked its end of day message at 16:00.

Most of the paper tape that we had produced lay on the floor in front of our table. On our instructor's orders, we severed the half-inch wide paper tape just after our last Morse print, rolled it into a tight bobbin and secured it with a small elastic band to be kept in our locker for tomorrow's lecture.

"I shall expect you to learn your Morse-alpha and numerals by heart as soon as you can. See you tomorrow," were his parting words.

As we walked into the classroom the next morning, each desk had a full page of typing for our next exercise, so we went to it and started our Morse keying. Our instructor went to each table to discuss our previous day's work tapes with each of us and finished with that job just before coffee break.

"Listen up everyone," he said after our break, "You all had the initial feel of what it means to key and each of you had a bit of advice on your handy work. From now on each of you will be timed as to your word speed, so make sure that your words and characters are spaced correctly, if not, your timing will show it. Your timing will also show up your knowledge of the alphabet, as looking at your alpha list will slow you down considerably."

We increased our speed for the first week, accuracy and neatness.

Beginning our second week, he made us listen to his transmissions and write down what we made of it. Although he keyed at a slow speed, we were taken by surprise at how difficult it was to get the instant recognition of a Morse character and write it down, thus falling behind constantly and starting again, etc. He stopped, smiled, and said: "This also needs training over and over again. I have tickertapes that each of you can place on your recorder. Take off your paper reel and put on your tickertape reel and clip the tape into your tickertape reader, switch on and put on your headphones. The speed of your tickertape can be set on your reader. Good listening!" So, we helped ourselves to a ticker tape and set to work. (This is like swimming. You can be told how to swim, but until you do it, you are in danger of drowning.)

The second week was devoted to gaining speed and accuracy to both our transmission rates, and our receiving capabilities. We took it in turn; before lunch break sending, and in the afternoon hours transmitting; or vice versa. Some of us stayed after the normal working day. Otherwise, it seemed that all of us got on fine, reaching speeds of up to ten or twelve words per minute. But somehow, that speed seemed to be a ceiling. It was hard to increase, like a mental block. But we constantly received encouragement and a good word of advice from our instructor, if he thought you really tried.

The third week was devoted to sending and receiving messages between us, using our table number as our call sign.

We were divided into groups of two, which our instructor changed from time to time. He also introduced atmospheric noises into our system At times, that made it hard to receive. But all by all, we seemed to progress nicely.

The last straws seemed backbreaking. We were mentally straining to get the last ounce of speed of receiving the stream of dots and dashes against a background of atmospheric noises. But our instructor showed no mercy! Transmitting Morse code was considered to be easier than receiving until you heard him say: "Utter rubbish. Nobody can understand that clicking noise. Slow down a bit. Reception, reception; reception by the receiving station, is all that counts! Do not show off! If you are slow, your experienced receiving station will come down to your level. You should show the same courtesy to other stations!"

dot dot dot–dash dash dash–dot dot dot
S–O–S
SAVE–OUR–SOULS

The international distress Morse signal until 1977. By radio telephone the distress signal is MAYDAY. It is alleged to derive from the French *m'aidez*; help me.

Our Morse code instructor at the Lord's Cricket Ground requested us to be quiet and said, "We have just received your movement orders. The British Royal Navy chaps have all been promoted to officer cadets and will now remove their black hat band and replace them with a white band. These will be supplied to you at the Naval Clothing Store on receipt of your voucher. You can collect your voucher from me just now. Further, our Royal Netherlands Navy friends have been transferred to the Sixty Third Observer Course at the Royal Naval Air Station to wait for HMS Condor, in Angus, Scotland at the nearest railway station Arbroath. Report for duty on October 1, 1943. No tropical island of Trinidad for you lovelies. What a shame! Oh well, you'll get over it!"

Our instructor then handed each of us an official looking envelope. What a surprise!

Note here that the normal sailor's uniform in the Royal Netherlands Navy has a blue collar with a white front, unlike the British sailor's uniform which is all blue. Both have the distinguishing three white bands round the rim of the collar. But our white front of the collar, made people think that that was the rank sign for officer cadets. We did not tell anyone, in case we were regarded as just common sailors. We got away with it and were regarded as equals in this militaristic world of rank distinction. It was quite silly, looking at it now!

The outcome of this was that, on the evening of September 30, 1943, all twelve of us found ourselves in a military transport vehicle at the colonnade of Euston Railway Station. After parking we were directed by Military Policeman to our train. We lugged our big kit bags to a platform where another Military Policeman directed us to the front coach of the waiting train. It was getting dark and there was a small guiding light. We had to be careful not to fall over baggage or into people. Eventually, we found our two reserved compartments in the front coach. In we clattered with our heavy kit bags, dragging them through the corridor, and heaving them into the two luggage racks. We sat down with some looking out the windows.

It was now dark here under the enormous station dome of shaped steel girders and glass panes. We all sat quietly, each to his own thoughts. Suddenly, the door was pushed open and two Royal Naval Reserve sub lieutenants stood in the dark corridor/ At the same time the locomotive gave a whistle and the train rolled slowly forward. We were asked by one of the officers if we could accommodate them. So we shifted a bit and made room for them in two opposite seats near the door.

As the train moved slowly out of the station, from the gloom into the dimness of the night, and we could see each other more clearly, the officer's voice came out, "How the hell did you get into the first class, you Sailors should be in third class with the rest of them?"

One of the sailors replied, "These two compartments are reserved for the Royal Naval Cadet Fleet Air Arm Observer's Training Course on HMS Condor, sir."

"Oh, I say, that's rich. Show me your travel warrants," said the officer.

Then the door was pushed open by a Military Policeman who said, "Travel Warrants, please."

And the two officers, sitting nearest to the door, handed theirs to the Military Policeman, who studied them with a torch and said, "You should not be in this compartment. Please remove yourselves from here. I'll deal with you later on." Then he checked all our warrants and smilingly said, "You're all right. Goodnight," and pushed the door closed. We sighed with relief!

We got our sandwiches and thermos flasks with hot tea, which were supplied to us by the NAAFI Ladies at the Lord's Cricket Ground. We ate our meal in the dark, looking out of the window into a night landscape as the train clickety clicked its way through the sleeping countryside. Not a single light was seen for mile after mile. We made a plan: one of us would sleep on the floor and the other five could stretch their legs out and rest them on the opposite seat. The shortest slept on the floor so the long-legged chaps could stretch out. We slept.

"Watford, Watford; all out for Watford," was the loud voice outside, repeating its message, over and over again. The locomotive was a huffing and a puffing at idle.

We stretched ourselves and yawned and someone stood at the window and said something about seeing stars, but no one was really listening. Then we felt the train slowly moving forward until it settled down to a regular beat, gaining speed and singing its normal clickety-click, clickety-click for miles on end.

We felt a need to visit the toilet and opened the compartment door to the corridor. But the corridor was full of sleeping bodies lying on the floor. You had to step very carefully over them to get to the end of the coach to the toilet. There was a queue. Coming near the toilet was a test of your olfactory nerves. The toilet door was jammed permanently open; there was no privacy! It seemed the railways could hardly cope with the demands to supply adequate sanitation and a degree of comfort to the mass movement of forces. Everybody took these conditions with good humor and the odd wisecrack. It was another kind of relief to finally get back in your seat!

The clickety-click song of a speeding train soon put us into a slumbering sleep. It went like this all night, from station to station. Luckily there were only about four stations. Then the train slowed down as we passed through a big town in the early morning and entered Edinburgh Station after an approximate eight-hour ride. We were stiff and tired and sat quietly for a while. We knew that part of this train would go further up the coast to Aberdeen.

A Royal Naval Military Policeman came in and told us to stay where we were. Another locomotive and the front three coaches would carry on up the coast. We had at least half an hour to ourselves and he advised us to try the NAAFI Canteen for a bite and a cuppa. Our gear would be safe as the train was guarded by Military Policeman. Why not? So we all moved to the Canteen and were warmly received by girls in their NAAFI uniforms.

They served us with a slice of the yellowish NAAFI cake and a cup of tea, after which we felt better. We enjoyed the company of the girls, until a Naval Military Policeman called us back to reality. We all took turns to visit the station toilets to have a bit of a wash.

The twelve of us were back on our seats in our two compartments and our new shorter train was slowly huffing and puffing out of Edinburgh Station heading northwards towards the Highlands; the land originally populated by the Picts, the ancient painted and tattooed people of unknown origin who existed long ago. It was now a little after eight hundred hours on October 1st, and the weather looked fine for a change as we were approached the famous bridge over the Firth of Forth.

The train thundered over this enormous steel bridge, built high above the water, giving us a clear view of the opposite coastline. We turned sharply to the east, stopped at Kirkcaldi, Dundee and then followed the coastline. At about ten hundred hours we entered Arbroath station. A naval transport bus took us to the Royal Naval Air Station HMS Condor.

Arbroath

Arbroath, in the Gaelic language, Obair Bhrothaig, or in the Scottish language, Aberbrothock, had a wartime population of eighteen thousand people. It lies on the North Sea coast around seventeen miles northeast of Dundee and fifty-one miles South of Aberdeen at an approximate longitude of three degrees west of the zero longitude of Greenwich, London. It lies approximately at latitude of fifty-seven degrees north of the Equator.

Arbroath is famous as the home of the Declaration of Arbroath, the statement of Scottish Independence, signed by nobility in 1320 and addressed to the Pope. It eulogized the services of their Lord and Sovereign Robert the Bruce. It has a fishing harbor and the town is famous for its local delicacy, the Arbroath Smokie. This is a kind of smoked haddock and a cottage industry that was exported worldwide.

RHMS Condor

This Royal Naval Air Station lay approximately three miles from Arbroath. Its airfield was covered in grass except for a very short section of tarmac landing strip which was made up to look like the flight deck of an aircraft carrier. The main structures, such as the staff quarters, the administration block, workshops, classrooms, the control tower and the gate house, were all made of plaster covered brick under slate roofs. The aircraft hangars were all constructed out of metal girders and corrugated plating with large sliding doors. The trainees were all housed in Nissenhuts which were prefabricated semi cylindrical shelters of arched corrugated iron sheets.

As we arrived at the main gate, properly called the Guard House, all twelve of us were given a registration form to complete with our personal details. We were told that from now on we would be called leading airman. We were led to our Nissenhuts, where we met other trainees. We learned that the Sixty Third Observer Course was roughly sixty men strong. There were twelve bunks in each Nissenhut, six bunks on each side and two pot belly coal stoves in the middle, roughly one third of the length of the hut from each other. Each coal stove was placed on a small cement floor, had its own coal scuttle and shovel and a small wood chopper. The six bunks in the middle of the hut were already occupied by the chaps that were there first. I was quite happy with one of the end bunks and threw my kitbag on it.

Each bunk had a tall steel clothes locker with its own key. I started unpacking my kit bag, when a loud voice shouted, "Attention!" I saw a petty officer at the door at the other end of the hut.

When everyone had quieted down and stood to attention, the voice at the door said, "Stand easy and listen up! I am Petty Officer Mackintosh, in charge of these ten Nissenhuts. Everybody in this establishment calls me Petty Officer Mac, and you may also call me that. Now, listen up carefully; these huts will be inspected by the Officer of the Watch at any time he wishes to do so. If he has the slightest complaint, the orderlies of that particular hut will be in serious trouble! Do I make myself clear?"

He took a long deep breath before going on and saying, "Two orderlies will be detailed to work for one week, starting with the chaps in the first two opposing bunks on this side, and the next week by the chaps in the next two opposing bunks, so each of you will have orderly duties for one week every other six weeks." He took a long deep breath and then said, "The orderlies are responsible for the hut to be kept neat, tidy, clean and quiet, no rowdiness will be tolerated, so each of you will obey their requests for assistance. The orderly duties are on this form pinned to the main door. I suggest that you read them carefully! Get yourselves unpacked, organized and settled in. Carry on!" he finished and walked out.

These Nissenhuts had no insulating material. All that was between us and the outside were the arched corrugated metal sheets from which these huts were made so the nights were chilly inside the hut and we hated to think what the winter nights would be like. In the meantime, we made the best of it with our greatcoat and warm socks we had and with our bunk blankets which seemed adequate.

The next day, we were all called out to the apron in front of one of the hangars. For the first time we saw the size of our Sixty Third Observer Course. There were fifty-five trainees and eleven instructors. We were introduced to the commander and his staff of this Royal Naval Air Station. One of the Swordfish aircraft was then pushed onto the apron and a group photograph was taken to commemorate this occasion.

The fifty-five trainees were divided into six separate study groups; groups A to F, we were group B. The three Dutch trainees were kept together, which we appreciated. We were introduced to the instructors who were divided into their technical expertise: Signals, Navigation, Flying, Weapons, Security, and Meteorology. Each study group shown around the Air Station and shown the classrooms, the control tower, the different hangars, and other buildings. We were told that every notice board would be provided on Sunday nights with the following week's detailed training

program. This week's was already on the notice boards; so we better
had a good look at them!

The three Dutch trainees were in the same Nissenhut in bunks
at the end of the hut near each other. Taco van Tijn had his bunk
next to mine and Remmert Aten was opposite mine at the end of the
hut.

The next day would really be the start of our training and
we were all looking forward to it in anticipation.

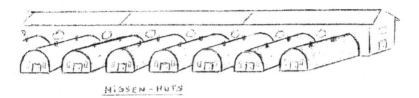

NISSEN - HUTS

PART 7—UP & AWAY

"When once you have tasted flight, you will forever
walk the earth with your eyes turned skywards"
Leonardo Da Vinci

Inception

Signals

On the third day we had Signals all morning as the first instruction period for our B group. Our instructor informed us that we would be given all the time required to turn us into competent and accomplished Morse signalmen as our job and lives would depend on it! This meant an extension to the time we had spent at Lord's Cricket Ground. Also, signaling with hand-held flags, semaphore, and a certain amount of fleet flag signals, which would come in useful with our convoy duties. From now on, we were scheduled for a couple hours every week to raise our skill level in Signals, mainly in Morse code. This would include the sessions in which our Signals Report from the Control Tower would be discussed, reflecting critically on our flying exercises.

Navigation

All afternoon was devoted by our navigating instructor, an RNVR lieutenant who carried Observers Wings, to a synopsis of the Fleet Air Arm's navigational practices.

The navigator does not bother with map technicalities, such as the type, Mercator or Conic, or the scale as suitable maps or charts would be supplied by the Admiralty.

Provided a reasonably small area of the earth is considered, it could be treated without great error as a flat or plane surface. The maps provided by the Admiralty, for convoy-escort duties, neglects spherical details and uses plane trigonometrically ratios only, treating the area as a flat surface, known as plane flying.

Most flying from aircraft carriers is away from land. The map is a blank piece of paper as the wide-open sea or ocean is devoid of landmarks and thus of map references. When flying near or toward land, landmarks appear on the map.

This type of navigation is known as dead reckoning navigation. Basically, it consists of navigating an aircraft using knowledge of the speed, heading and height of the aircraft and a knowledge of the wind direction and velocity in order to arrive at the desired destination.

A land-based air station or airport is stationary; but an aircraft carrier moves away from its position where you took off. Because it is wartime, your carrier is not allowed to communicate its or the fleet's change of course and speed. This means that on your return, at your ETA (Estimated Time of Arrival), you may not find your carrier. This is especially difficult in bad weather which forces you to make a search for it. Constant accurate track keeping is essential!

We were provided with a sort of mechanical computer which was strapped just above the right knee, or left knee if left-handed. It was designed to solve vector-triangle problems, such as track, heading and wind-vector-triangle pro problems, without having to plot them.

Our instructor mentioned some technical terms which would be fully explained at future lectures such as; track = the line of travel, velocity = direction together with speed. Thus, a wind-velocity could be ninety degrees at twenty knots.

Vector = one of the lines in a two-dimensional geometrical figure. Thus, you can refer to a vector-triangle or a vector parallelogram or simply a line having a fixed length and direction but no fixed position.

Bearing = the direction in which any point lies from a reference point, which could be from your position. Normally expressed in degrees from a compass reading, a compass bearing or expressed in clock face hours, with twelve o'clock being dead ahead.

Position = a place occupied by a thing. Reporting your position in terms of latitude and longitude is frowned upon in the military or the navy for security reasons. You can give your position by giving bearing and distance from a known or predetermined reference point. All of these were given in a typed list for us to study. Last but not least, our instructor showed us the Chart or Plotting Board and the mechanical computer which we would be provided. The Plotting Board was about twenty-four inches by twenty-four inches in size. It had a moving arm with a parallel ruler attached to it. The whole contraption was contained in a canvas bag for easy carrying. Luckily, it was not bulky, as it had to be used and handled in a small cockpit. All this was food for thought as we left the classroom to return to our Nissenhut, our home from home.

For the rest of the week we had the same lectures, Morse in the morning and navigation after lunch which we found very interesting as it dealt in great detail with relative wind, wind finding, and drift. We all looked forward to getting to put it into practice.

Requisites

On Monday morning of our second week at HMS Condor, nature and the weather were autumnal. Our two potbellied stoves were lit every afternoon after our daily duties and kept going throughout the night. Every Nissenhut had its own coal box and tinder wood box outside which were replenished from time to time by Air Station's staff.

Our orderly duty was to fill two scuttles, bring in tinder wood and start the fires every afternoon after lectures. From now on there always had to be at least one person in the hut as long as the fires were burning. This was usually one of the orderlies who tended the stoves. Some were near the stoves and others, like the three Dutchmen, were furthest away. They needed an extra blanket but it all worked out fine. Luckily, we did not have many snorers. The loudest were soon sorted out tender shouts or the odd shoe! It all worked out with the usual sailor's humor. We had to live in peace together!

In our Signals lecture room the next morning, instead of our Morse teacher was a Lieutenant RNVR with pilot wings on his sleeve. He introduced himself as Lieutenant Mings. He took roll, ticked us off on his clipboard and informed us that this morning we would be fitted with our flying togs in the stores and requested that we follow him.

In stores we were given a form listing all the gear we would receive for which we had to sign and were told to make sure that we received what was on the list.

We received: Flying underwear consisting of two white silk overalls, to be worn next to the skin; two long woolen underpants and two long sleeved woolen vests, a flying jacket of soft brown leather, fur lined with a big fur collar, flying helmet of soft brown leather with two earphones permanently attached and with their long connecting lead. We got a face mask which had to be clipped and plugged onto the flying helmet. It covered the nose and mouth with a microphone permanently attached in front of the mouth. We also received; flying gloves with large cuffs of fleece lined soft brown leather and two white cotton hand gloves. These gloves had four leather thongs to attach to our gloves and worn round the neck as navigators normally took their gloves off when plotting. We got flying overalls with leg pockets and pencil holders on the sleeves and our yellow May West lifejacket. We got a flight navigator's calculator and flight navigator's notepad, both with leg straps; a navigator's wristwatch; binoculars in a leather box; long, thick, white woolen socks, thereby hangs a tale; fleece-lined flying boots, which reached to our knees; and a navigator's parachute harness.

We had to try them all on/ We looked and waggled like overstuffed bears much to everyone's mirth! When we all signed our official list and were given a copy, everything was marked with nametags. A van was loaded with them and driven to our Nissenhut.

Lieutenant Mings got the NAAFI girls to make a pot of coffee for us which was most appreciated. We all fussed about sorting out our new flying gear, folding them and stowing them all away into our lockers.

The navigator in his open cockpit of a Swordfish aircraft was not strapped down into his seat, like his pilot. He sat on a small seat to do his plotting and at times, stand up to take a bearing or search the ocean or take a photograph or man the gun and had to be free to move. To prevent him from being thrown overboard by a sudden movement of his aircraft, up, down or sideways, he was tethered to the floor by a Monkey Tail. This was a strong length of webbing clipped to the floor at one end and to the navigator's harness between his legs on the other end. The navigator had to carry his parachute by hand and stow it into his cockpit. When in need he had to clip it onto his harness on his chest.

After lunch, we had our navigation lecture. It was now given by a chief petty officer who carried a Bearing Compass; the type of compass used by navigators.

Note: The word direction can be confusing. Wind direction is indicated by the direction from which the wind is blowing because that is the direction the weather is coming from. But a tidal stream or current, electric or liquid, always moves in the direction to which it is flowing.

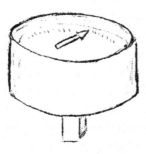

BEARING COMPASS

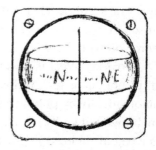

STEERING COMPASS

There were two types of compass, the magnetic compass and the gyrocompass. Owing to technical difficulties in the 1940s, a satisfactory gyroscopic compass was not yet employed in the older British Naval aircraft, so the magnetic compass remained in use.

There were two types of magnetic compass; the steering and the bearing type. The difference was in the way they were read.

The steering type was read horizontally. You looked at a vertical strip dial straight ahead with the lubber's line indicating the direction of the aircraft's heading. The lubber's line is a vertical line inside the compass case, behind which the compass vertical strip dial rotates.

The bearing type compass has a horizontal circular compass dial showing the full three hundred and sixty degrees divided into degrees of arc in a clockwise direction. It is read by looking down on it. The compass card also shows the cardinal points of North, East, South and West and the four Quadrants North East, South East, South West and North West. In air navigation, the general practice is to indicate the value of the compass reading in a three-figure notation of degrees of arc, such as forty-five degrees for NE or one hundred eighty degrees for South.

Magnetic compasses are reliable on the straight and level, but unreliable when the aircraft makes steep turns, accelerates, decelerates, dives, and makes sudden changes. This demands close cooperation between pilot and navigator.

Then we dealt with such topics as Heading, Bearing, Track and Track Angle, their differences, their meridian angles and the mistakes one must avoid. These are technical details and I will not bore you with them.

A May West is a wonderful bright yellow colored lifejacket. It is not an actual jacket but a vest which can be blown up automatically by pulling a short cord near the bottom of the vest or by blowing it up by mouth through a rubber tube. Near its shoulder is a bag of fluorescent greenish yellow dye which will color the sea around you to make you more visible from the air. There is also a small pocket which holds a small box with two hypodermic needles to inject a strong painkiller, morphine. Fixed to one of the shoulders is a red light which automatically switches on as soon as you hit the sea. Another pocket contains an emergency ration; chocolate bars full of energy giving glucose and other goodies. On the left chest is a fixed sheath holding a sharp knife with a round top to prevent accidental holes in your rubber dinghy or your May West. At the back near the armpit is a small first-aid kit. Last is a police whistle to attract attention if your voice has gone. It looks like a lot of stuff, but it is so neatly arranged and well thought out that it is hardly noticeable.

Knitting for Victory

That evening after our duties, we took a good look at the flying clothes we received, and an animated discussion ensued about them until one of the men shouted, "Look at this. It's unbelievable. Look in your white woolen socks." Out little folded pieces of writing paper, which had a written message on them. "For my brave flyer, with all my love. Please contact me at such and such address." Some had red lipstick lip marks on them.

How to drop a 'fish

Some messages made us blush and some were very nice and sweet. But nearly all wanted to be contacted. Some were from older women who wrote something sad about their son or husband they had lost. It was an amazing experience to all of us and the mood in the hut went very quiet with each of us thinking of our own family.

Our War Chariot

We were now beginning of our third week at HMS Condor and had done quite well with our Morse communication, had interesting navigational lectures and were now entering our flying instructions.

In one of the hangars we were shown our war chariot, the Fairey Swordfish MKII, officially classified as a Torpedo Bomber Reconnaissance. She was lovingly known as the Stringbag. She was 10.9 meters in length, 4 meters in height, and had a wingspan of 13.9 meters. She looked far bigger than we had imagined. Her further statistics were: an air-cooled nine-cylinder radial 750hp Bristol Pegasus engine, a top speed of 224 kph, armament consisting of two .303 machineguns, one six hundred and eighty-one kg torpedo and eight 27 kg rockets. When not carrying a torpedo, she could carry mines, bombs or a big depth charge up to her maximum carrying capacity. The Swordfish was a biplane with wing struts between the wings and thin steel wires tightened between them to give rigidity and strength. This is the reason why she is nicknamed Stringbag. There were good reasons for having biplanes in those early days of aircraft carrier work in the Fleet Air Arm as they could land at lower speeds, a useful attribute at sea. The wings folded against the aircraft body to take less deck space than monoplanes which needed a greater wingspan to achieve the same lift and carry the same load.

However, their slow speeds 195 kph when carrying a load made them vulnerable to anti-aircraft fire during their low and long steady approach on a target when delivering their torpedoes.

The Swordfish was built to take three men; a pilot, a navigator and a telegraphist/gunner. However, the tele-graphist/gunner was often left out to increase flying time and distance. Also, they had to carry an extra fuel tank in the cockpit or extra electronic equipment or increase carrying capacity.

Note: The picture above shows the three cockpits. The pilot's panel can be seen in the front; the navigator's cockpit in the middle shows the two small bulges on each side which are Bearing Compass mounts.

An Arrestor Hook was fitted to the rear fuselage to enable the Swordfish to make deck landings. It is interesting to note that the fuselage construction between the Arrestor Hook and the engine mount has to be strong enough to withstand the enormous deceleration forces when the Arrestor Hook catches the arrestor wire on landing. This stops the aircraft from a speed of some ninety-five kph nearly instantly.

If the aircraft is launched off by catapult, acceleration force comes into play. The pilot is well strapped into his seat, but the navigator is not and has to brace himself in time.

If anyone can lay claim to the origins of the Fairey Swordfish (Fairey is the builder and designer of the Swordfish), it is the Greek Naval Air Arm. As early as 1932, the Fairey Technical Department received a specification for a Greek Naval Torpedo Bomber. This resulted in the Swordfish in April 1935. By then, the Greeks had lost interest but Fairey went on with this project. Prototypes were flown and tested from the privately owned Fairey airfield, known as the Great West Aerodrome. This later became London's Heathrow Airport.

Swordfish were also built by the Blackburn Company and called Blackfish.

Historical Achievements and Hardships

The Swordfish was just an airplane; its legends and achievements were only as good as the skilled crews made them. Some examples of these are given next.

Atlantic Convoys

Atlantic Convoys of twenty to eighty ships plied the Atlantic to Murmansk, North Russia, to Halifax, Nova Scotia. Canada or to New York. German U-Boats, working in packs, were a real menace, sinking hundreds of ships in mid ocean.

The North Atlantic Ocean in the best of times was rough, but appalling in winter with temperatures below freezing, spray and snow freezing as it fell on the flight deck with heavy sea swells, thick clouds and visibility less than half a mile. Serviceability remained high and flying crews on patrols often gambled on whether they would get back. When they did they had to be lifted, frozen, from their open cockpits. The Escort Carriers and later on the Merchant Aircraft Carriers carrying Swordfish and Wildcat fighters answered this menace and destroyed many U-Boats.

Toranto, Italy

November 11, 1940

Twenty-one Swordfish aircraft took off from the aircraft carrier HMS Illustrious in two separate strikes that night; twelve Swordfish in the first strike and nine in the second, approximately half an hour later. They sunk three Italian Battleships; the Conte di Cavour, the Littorio and the Caio Duilio; they badly damaged three Trento class Cruisers; set fire to the Toranto harbor fuel tanks; bombed ships and a store depot and set the seaplane base on fire. This was all done in one night with the loss of two Swordfish with two flyers taken prisoner. This virtually ended Italian naval actions in the Mediterranean.

Bismarck

May 26, 1941

Just before 20:00 hours on a rain soaked gusty evening, fifteen Swordfish from the carrier HMS Ark Royal, attacked the new fifty-thousand-ton German battleship Bismarck.

At that time, the Bismarck was the largest, state-of-the-art battleship afloat with her eight, three hundred and eighty mm guns, twelve, one hundred and fifty mm guns, as well as scores of one hundred and five mm ack-ack guns and a host of close range armament. She also had the latest radar gun-aiming gear, armored with decks up to one hundred and twenty mm thick and a cruising speed of twenty-nine knots. Two Swordfish attack the Bismarck from the starboard quarter. They plummeted to skim the heaving water, finally flying so low that fire from the Bismarck's guns passed over them. One of the Swordfish delivered a crippling torpedo before it banks and climbs away. Below water, near its stern, Bismarck is pierced by this torpedo. The explosion damages the steering gear and the maimed giant careers in circles, making easy prey for British warships to pound her to destruction and sink her.

All this was news to me. It made me realize that although the Swordfish was an out of date aircraft and looked a bit old fashioned, it certainly could deliver a knock-out punch in well-planned and executed operations.

Up and Away

This part of our course was directed at Fleet Air Arm flying personnel to make us appreciate what our contribution and sacrifice would mean to the overall benefit of the British Isles in particular and the Allies in general. Our lecturer was a pukka straight ringed Royal Naval lieutenant who addressed us in impeccable English with an aristocratic naval accent. He put at ease all fifty-five of us in one of the hangars. His lecture gave us an historical background of the titanic struggle in which Britain was badly mauled by German U-Boats.

The Royal Navy and the RAF Coastal Command had been forged by Churchill's instruction into a single assemblage known as Western Approaches. They were installed at Liverpool and under the operational control of the Admiralty in London. Western Approaches would control all shipping; mercantile, naval or private and direct their movements either in convoy or singly. They would gather intelligence on enemy shipping and U-Boat movements; prepare weather reports, and generally assist shipping and give guidance and protection, where possible, in the whole of the Atlantic Ocean: thus the Western Approaches to the British Isles. Their work slowly reduced the losses of shipping and made it very difficult and hazardous for German U-Boats to operate.

Our lecturer gave statistical figures to impress on us the seriousness of the frightful fall in imports which could potentially be a mortal danger.

He concluded by saying, "Although you may perceive yourself to be a small cog in a vast clockwork, your dexterity and skill in the work and activities in which you are very soon to exercise will contribute to our final victory. We wish you God's speed!"

This lecture took us to almost lunch-time and allowed us to study the notice board before going into the canteen. To our surprise the three Dutchmen were to report to the Commander Flying's office after lunch break.

169

We waited for him in the reception area until we were called into his office. After having put us at ease he said, "Well chaps your time for flying has come. Have any of you been up in an aircraft? No? Well you will do so, weather permitting, in the next three days in an amphibian seaplane taking off from the Firth of Forth. This type of plane is the Super marine Walrus or simply Walrus. It is mainly used for Air-Sea-Rescue and for laying parachute mines in enemy waters. They are stationed near the Firth of Forth Railway Bridge just south of Dunfirmline. We will take you there in a van so be ready by 08:00 hours at the Guard House. You may travel in your naval battle-dress. I wish our Navy had those! Just take your flying jacket, which you may wear; helmet and your flying gloves. I suggest that you carry your flying boots and socks in a handbag as they can become very hot and sweaty if you wear them. The Walrus has a closed cockpit, so you'll be all right. Any questions?"

We were too gob-smacked to think of anything to ask, so he smiled and wished us an interesting and pleasant experience and we were dismissed.

At 08:00 hours we presented ourselves at the Guard House. We were given our travel warrants and signed ourselves out in the liberty book.

A WAAF (Woman Auxiliary Air Force) Motor Transport driver was patiently waiting for us in van. She told us that she would take us to the Walrus Station. She said, "Please call me Ann." We introduced ourselves, jumped into the van and off we went.

Note: With Spitfire fighters giving top cover and FW190 German fighters attacking, this picture shows a downed fighter pilot in his dingy, being rescued under fire, by a Walrus.

With Spitfire fighters giving top cover and
FW190 German fighters attacking, this picture shows a downed
fighter pilot in his dingy, being rescued under fire, by a Walrus.

Coastal trip to the Walrus Station.

We turned left on to the road to Arbroath as we came out of the
Main Gate of HMS Condor, then were on to the road from Aberdeen
to Edinburg via Dundee. We all spoke in English; Ann with a
Scottish accent while our English must have had a very foreign
accent.

"Please speak Dutch," said Ann, "I've never heard that
language spoken," so we did from time to time.

"To you this must sound like Double Dutch?" I said to her.
Ann never answered my remark as she was going round a corner
when she suddenly had to break heavily to avoid an accident with
an oncoming car cutting the corner at speed. It tried to avoid Ann's
van but failed and scraped our van along the side making an awful
noise. Ann stopped the van but the other driver over-steered and
toppled over in a maddening turn.

Ann was slumped over her steering wheel, trembling and
sobbing a little. While Taco attended to her, Remmert and I jumped
out of our van to help the people in the other car. We found one

male driver who was thrown clear of his car on to the grassy side of the road. We found him just coming out of a state of unconsciousness with some blood trickling out of his hair. Remmert shouted to Ann asking her if she had a first-aid kit. Luckily, she did. Taco found it and threw it across the road. Remmert caught it and attended to the casualty by stopping the bleeding with a tight bandage round his head while I switched off his engine.

At that moment, another naval van with a WAAF Motor Transport driver stopped and asked if she could be of assistance. Our driver Ann got out to talk to her colleague. She asked her to go to the nearest phone and report the accident to HMS Condor. She was on her way in no time at all, speeding off down the road towards Arbroath.

We covered our casualty with two of our flying jackets to keep him warm and put one of our thick woolen flying socks under his head for comfort. Once fully conscious, we told him to lie quite still until further medical help arrived.

Ann's naval van looked a real mess on the side. Taco stayed with Ann; Remmert stayed with his casualty; while I stayed at the roadside to attend to traffic.

Private public transport in war time was very scarce as petrol rationing was severe unless you had an official logbook for supplementary rations. Persons such as doctors, taxi drivers, delivery vans, long haul drivers, transport carriers or lorries had special rations to fit their requirements.

After a while I heard the faint siren of an ambulance in the distance coming quickly towards us. They arrived and told us that the police were on the way as well as another naval van and driver. The police from Arbroath arrived on the scene and collected all the necessary information from Ann and us. They took Ann back to HMS Condor.

Ann's replacement, also a WAAF Motor Transport driver, said, "Please call me Martha." She took us to our destination at the Walrus Naval Air Station.

All this was just a diversion, but it had shaken us a bit. Now we were starving and ready for lunch! We nearly forgot our two flying jackets and woolen sock, but Martha had sweetly asked if we had all our gear. This started a mutual finger-pointing exercise between the three of us while Martha quietly dropped our gear, started the van and drove away waving to us!

We went through the usual arrival routine at the Guard House. We were shown to our quarters, which consisted of two double-decker wooden bunks in a small brick building near the Guard House that housed other sailors.

Lunch break was announced by the Tannoy. We were shown to the canteen by a sailor who had popped out of midair, apparently sent to look after us. We entered the canteen and joined the queue leading to the trough. "What's that?" I must look it up in the dictionary; something to do with food?

We took trays and waited our turn. Some sailors asked what or who we were, so we told them and made friends for life! That was the short of it.

After we were served, our sailor friends invited us to their table. We must have eaten ravenously as our new friends let us eat after which the questions came. We answered as well as we could.

The Tannoy clicked on: "The three newly arrived leading airmen to report to Sub Lieutenant Robinson at the main hanger with their flying clothes."

We rushed back to our quarters, collected our flying togs and found Sub Lieutenant Robinson, with the help of one of our new friends. We were all out of breath and felt a bit silly!

"Where is the fire?" was his friendly greeting. "My name is Mike Robinson and I'm your pilot for today. You are here with the Seven Hundred and Fifty-First Squadron. Our main mission is Air Sea Rescue but when called on we lay mines, do reconnaissance along the coast and, as of now, take Trainee Airmen for a ride allowing them to practice their exercises. Today we will show you how to detect and determine your drift as you were taught. Who has flown before? Nobody. I'm sure you will like it. You can call me

Mike once we're in the air. Put on your flying-jacket and helmet and your flying boots and leave your shoes somewhere in the hangar. I will take two of you-at-a time, one as an observer sitting next to me to do his exercise. The other mans the radio and keeps us in contact with our station."

Our Walrus was already off the slipway moored to two buoys. We decided that Taco and I would go first. We went down the slipway to a sailor holding a rubber boat. We got in and were rowed to our Walrus where two other sailors were waiting for us. Our pilot scrambled up the side quickly. We were shown where the footholds were. Taco went before me and consequently was the first to walk into the radio operator's position inside this flying boat. I had the seat next to the pilot, the normal position for the navigator or the co-pilot.

The pilot looked back to Taco and shouted that all Taco had to know to handle the radio was in a file on his desk; call signs and what to say, "Oh, yes, I forgot to tell you. We are on Radio/Telephony, so there is no need for Wireless/Telegraphy and no need to use Morse Signals.

That was something we were taught and that it was the latest electronic gadget used only by fighter pilots. All aircrafts would eventually have it; hopefully before the end of the war!

The pilot showed us where to plug-in our earphone jacks and started the engine with a loud bang which he told us was the starting cartridge. The three sailors in their rubber boat were patiently waiting at the front buoy to which the Walrus' bow was moored. At a sign from the pilot they slipped the rope freeing the bow. The pilot gave a bit more throttle pulling on the stern buoy and pulling the Walrus round to face open water while the sailors rowed to the stern buoy. On a sign from the pilot they slipped the stern rope and freed the Walrus.

"Are you all strapped in?" asked the pilot over the intercom. On our "Yes," opened the throttle. The engine roared louder as he navigated the Walrus to the open waters of the Firth of Forth.

He headed down the Firth of Forth giving it full throttle sending the Walrus bouncing and bumping over the water. It banged and slammed over the waves until majestically, the Walrus planed low over waves, given the odd smack by larger waves until it was gliding through the air. We slowly gained height and were flying with the engine roaring.

On October 20, 1943, I was airborne for the first time in my life! What a thrill! Up and away into the third dimension—a dream come true!

The Making of an Air Navigator

In retrospect, over the last five months, I was trained and instructed in how to behave on parade and in public as a Royal Naval person. Now to be capable of communicating in the world of Wireless Telegraphy using the Morse code and Radio Telephony, using the spoken word in the disciplined manner of the Radio Telephony code was great; I knew some basics of Air Navigation; getting to know my position in my designated weapon platform, the Royal Navy strike aircraft, the Fairey Swordfish.

Today I had my first airborne exercise and became a petty officer airman, one little step up from leading airman.

Note: These naval rank distinctions were from the British Royal Navy and not from our Royal Netherlands Navy. They were used to simplify the administration and organization.

Another distinction was that we were paid air hours while our British colleagues were not. We completed two identical navigator's logbooks for this purpose. From time to time, we would send one logbook to our naval headquarters in London to get paid for our air hours. This was a welcome extra or tip. We had one further distinction; our major handicap was the English language.

We often sat together until late at night making sense of what was said in the classroom. We could puzzle out technical details using our Dutch/ English dictionaries. Idioms, dialects, and vernacular were often not understood, not to mention indistinct or garbled speech such as the Army Major who spoke from behind his big moustache. He sounded like a pompom to us.

To give an example that demonstrates what is meant: follow the following conversation between the Air Control Tower and one of our chaps in the air. "Hello Tiger, this is Tiger Base, are you airborne, over?" Tiger's trainee navigator: "Hello Tiger Base, this is Tiger, hear you loud and clear, no I was born in Amsterdam, over and out."

Nevertheless, we overcame most of our difficulties and our pilots and instructors always tried to help! Even so, I perceived that we gave them a laugh a minute!

Now we came to a watershed. From now on we had to practice what we had learned in the classroom over and over. We had roughly seven months before we qualified and got our wings, so we had to pull out all the stops!

Over sixty years is a long time for my poor memory to remember details, so I referred to my navigator's logbook for all the exercises we had to carry out in the air in different types of aircraft. I spent forty-six air hours flying in the Walrus doing things like wind finding. There is a thing, not always fully appreciated by a landlubber. To find a wind on the ground, you wet your finger, stick it up in the air and the side that dries first is the direction from where the wind blows. But it does not give you the wind speed! Once you are up in the air, an accurate knowledge of the wind velocity, wind direction and wind speed, is of paramount importance.

The different altitudes at which you fly may have their own wind velocity which complicates things a bit. Thus, you have to watch changes all the time—like a hawk! I elaborate on this point for the simple reason that the wind pushes the aircraft in its flight. This is known as drift. As a result, the compass course which is the flight course, is not the track you follow over the sea or land. Many bombers and fighters have lost their bearings because of a drift they were not aware of. When low on petrol this is a great danger! Wind drift does not worry the landlubber, but to the airmen of my time it could be the difference between coming home or going down at sea or having to make a forced landing on land which could be enemy territory.

Another thing we did was use the early type of Radio Direction Finder. Later, advanced equipment became Radio Direction and Ranging, or RADAR. Thus, we spent hours flying in the Anson as a fully equipped flying RADAR lecture room for six trainees.

We did homing in exercises on ships or buoys, telling the pilot how to get to these targets by giving him courses to fly and finally telling him by words like, "Left-left" "right-right" or "steady as you go," talking him right over the target using the radar equipment. Thus, in thick fog we should be able to talk him to a target or to our own aircraft carrier and talk him to the right position to make a safe landing."

Other interesting exercises were with the Camera Gun, a big, bulky camera which we held hanging over the side at the end of our monkey-tail, the tether that held us on board, and took pictures. Another exercise was the Air-to-Air firing with our Lewis Gun on drogues pulled by other aircraft or on ground targets. The bulk of all our exercises were navigational to all sorts of destinations, meeting other aircraft in the air at a stipulated time, in all sorts of weather conditions, overland, over the sea and both, having to make a precise landfall and carrying out searches and square searches. We practiced what to do if lost or had instrument failure. We went to a large swimming pool to practice handling the large dinghy which was supposed to automatically pop out of the top wing when the aircraft hit the water in an emergency. We practiced how to work with our May West and use its contents and how to inject morphine to alleviate severe pain.

We had one accident which involved Remmert Aten. His pilot had his engine stall on him just south of Montrose. He had to make a forced landing on the railway track, snapping a couple of wooden telephone poles and breaking his under carriage. Otherwise both pilot and Remmert were unhurt.

Remmert and his pilot had to run down the railway line, one running north and the other one south, to place a flare on the track and wave an oncoming train to stop which they were able to do. We toasted them in the bar as all had gone well!

We did all these things in various aircraft, such as the Firefly, the Barracuda, the Anson, and the Walrus, but mostly the Swordfish. We were destined to join a Swordfish Squadron. These planes came from various second line squadrons.

Note: First line meant facing the enemy. Their three-digit Squadron number nearly always started with the numeral eight.

Second-line Squadrons did things like Air-Sea Rescue, Transport, Instructing, Ambulance work. Their three-digit Squadron number nearly always started with the numeral seven.

We worked hard these seven months; approximately two hundred day and fifteen night-flying hours and umpteen classroom hours. We did our finals on May 27, 1944. The Dutch group was told to report to RNAS Donibristle where a small Dutch administrative naval detachment would take over the control of our further movements.

PART 8—CREW TRAINING

"Ad utrumque paratus."
"Prepare to cope with every eventuality
including the final one."

What Next?

When the three of us stepped out of our Light Delivery Van which took us from RNAS HMS Condor to RNAS Donibristle, we saw a grass covered airfield which sloped very slightly towards the south. In the distance we saw the city of Edinburgh and the famous cantilever railway bridge that connected Edinburgh to the north side of the Firth of Forth. We also saw the Walrus Naval Air Station near the bridge and felt at home in this part of the world, both on land and from the air.

We went through the same routine of booking in. We observed with a keen eye that the place was well staffed with WRNS or Wrens (Woman's Royal Naval Service). This made Taco give me a wink. We wondered if Remmert had noticed! We were soon sorted and shown to a lieutenant of administration with his two silver stripes. (All officers of the Administrative Staff in the Royal Netherlands Navy wear a uniform with silver braiding and badges.) He made us welcome, ordered coffee and told us that we had to be in London, at our Royal Naval Headquarters as soon as possible. There was a night train on the Scotch Express and he had booked us on tonight's train! He told us to eat first and they would get us to the train on time!

Wow. That was the last thing we needed but there was a war on, so!

In their haste they were not able to book us a seat on the train. With our heavy kit bags and bits and pieces we would probably block the passageway on the coach. But the lieutenant was sure he could bribe us into the Guard luggage van. To our surprise, he did! Even so, we had an awful journey trying to sleep on the floor between heaps of luggage.

We arrived early in the morning at London's Euston Railway Station and were summarily chucked out of the luggage van. There we were, bleary-eyed, trying to get a trolley. Wherever we looked around us in this military multitude, trolleys were scarce as pigeon's teeth. Remmert Aten remarked that they were all at the front entrance to the station where they were abandoned after use. He volunteered to reconnoiter and off he went into the crowd. Remmert was a beanstalk, tall and slender built but wiry. When he came back, sticking out over the crowd with a triumphant smile on his face, he was followed by two Dutch Sailors each pulling a trolley behind them. Things went quickly, and we soon arrived at our RNN Headquarters.

We were ushered into the presence of Lieutenant Commander Witkamp, a two-and-a-half ringer, who put us at ease, offered us a seat and went on with his work. After a while he looked up, gave us a big smile and said, "As of yesterday, the first of June 1944, you three were officially appointed by Royal Decree to the rank of sub-lieutenant observer navigator which means that you are in the wrong uniform. Is that understood?"

We were dumbfounded and could only hoarsely whisper, "Yes sir."

"I did not hear that," he said cupping his hands over his ears.

"Yes, sir, understood!" we nearly shouted which made him laugh heartily.

"We have ordered three full sub-lieutenant uniform outfits from a shop in Regent Street called Simpson's. You have to go there to have your measurements taken and be fitted out. These uniforms will be finished soon but, in the meantime, get your naval battledress updated if they are still presentable. Otherwise get new ones. They can be supplied while you wait and all you will need in addition is your officer's cap. Off you go and come back to this office for further orders."

There we stood, telling Lieutenant Commander Witkamp that we did not know London and asked if someone could tell us how to get to Regent Street and if we could have some money? He produced three envelopes with money and said, "Good you asked. I will order a car for you to take you there and back."

All went well at Simpson's of Regent Street. The front shop window declared in large letters, *"From The Cap Down"* as their motto.

We arrived back at Lieutenant Commander Witkamp's desk dressed in our new battle dress with epaulettes with one gold braided stripe, our gold observer/navigator metal wing and medal and wearing our officer's cap. We had undergone a metamorphosis and our faces must have reflected that we were tickled pink or more formally: affected by a sense of pleasing excitement, or just plain proud and happy!

Lieutenant Commander Witkamp shook hands with us and continued, "We have booked you into Regents Park Hotel near Piccadilly Circus which will put you in a central position for underground trains, entertainment, bus services and what have you. Your luggage has already been placed in your rooms. You will also be near Simpson's. I suggest that you tell them where you are. Your salary has been increased. In the meantime, you'll have to do with what I've given you. Here's my card with this address and my phone number. Any questions?"

"Yes sir, what is going to happen to us?" we asked.

"Oh yes, from now on you are regarded as being first line. You will receive further training with live ordnance and realistic exercises. You are now on leave until further notice, enjoy it and be careful; London can be a wicked city if you let it be! Okay?"

We nodded, said "Sir," saluted, and departed to find our transport driver. At Regents Park Hotel each of us was shown to his own single room at the top floor, overlooking the rooftops of London. We hadn't had such luxury with its creature comforts for a long time!

What a transformation; we began by being paid and had to carry a pay book which doubled as an identity document. Now we received a salary by check and had a separate identity document. We had a top-quality number one uniform with an embroidered wing and a daily routine uniform with a metal pin-up wing, lovely white shirts and black tie, a stylish greatcoat, and such. We had to get used to all this. It was not difficult, but it was different!

While we were on leave we experienced a massive German bombardment. The details follow.

Vergelt Waffen literally means Reprisal Weapons and so they were: the V-1 and the V-2. The V-1 was known by its throbbing buzz like an old Model-T Ford going up a hill. It was known as the Buzz Bomb or Doodle-Bug. 6,725 reached England. 2,420 fell on London causing 6,000 deaths, and 18,000 badly injured. Severe and widespread damage played on people's nerves to a great extent with children being evacuated out of London.

The buzzing noise came from a simple but ingenious pulse jet engine that powered the V-1. It was a pilotless flying bomb with an 850 kg warhead. The most frightening characteristic was when the buzz abruptly stopped (people below held their breath) the projectile would go into a dive and fifteen seconds later hit the ground and exploded with an enormous noise, massive shockwave and destruction.

The first one came over London on June 13, 1944, while we were in London and could hear and sometimes feel their explosions from our top floor hotel room windows. We watched, mesmerized, seeing plumes of smoke rising up into the air from where they had fallen, randomly, day and night.

A V-2 rocket carried a one-ton warhead and fell silently without warning from a great height. They started falling on London on September 8, 1944. Altogether, 1,115 fell on Britain. 517 of them fell in the London area. They caused 2,754 deaths and 6,500 seriously injured.

While went on, nobody knew how long this hell would continue. In February 1945, V-2 bombs started falling on southern England where the Second Front on the Normandy Beach in France was being prepared; thousands of American troops were being amassed and the British government nearly panicked with Churchill ordering that all the detailed information on the V-bombs be kept secret to prevent serious unrest under a bewildered population. It was with great relief that the V-bombs stopped coming in March 1945.

Leave? What leave?

We were given travel warrants after only two days leave and told to report to RNAS Inskip in Lancaster on June 15, 1944. We travelled by train to Blackpool and then by Royal Naval transport to RNAS Inskip, some thirteen km east of Blackpool. We considered ourselves lucky to get out of the London area!

Number one Naval Operational Training Unit at RNAS Inskip, HMS Nightjar was a grass carpeted airfield with pleasant accommodations, workshops for armorers and aircraft fitters and some hangars. The different squadrons had their aircraft dispersed round the periphery of the airfield with light delivery vans to transport air crews or technicians and their tools to and from the central buildings.

We arrived in the late afternoon of June 15, 1944, and were cordially received by a Wren Officer who ushered us to our small, pleasant bedrooms. A big ginger tomcat awaited us with his tail straight up in the air giving us a friendly welcome "meow" and rubbing himself round our trouser legs which resulted in the Wren picking him up, stroking him, saying, "Hope you will enjoy your stay," and closing the door.

All my gear was neatly stacked in a corner of the room and I started to unpack and stack things in a wardrobe and a chest of drawers.

Hello Rego

The Tannoy told us it was supper time. Not knowing what to put on, I changed into my Number One, one and only, uniform with great pride. There was a knock on the door. I let in a Dutch pilot with neatly combed blond hair, slender and dressed in a neat navy-blue battledress with pilot wings. He said, "Hi, I'm Rego, and you must be Tip adoring himself in the mirror. Forget it. Battledress all the time but keep a clean and neat uniform ready for the wardroom." With that said he sat down on the bed.

I replied, "Hi yourself," and we shook hands. Rego said, "Get changed and we'll meet up in the bar; I'll buy you a drink. What's your poison?"

"Gin and tonic," I replied to a figure halfway through the door.

Hello Musketeers

The bar was spacious, well stocked, tax free, and had a pleasant atmosphere with Wren Stewardesses attending to our orders for which we signed. This was a cashless society. The bar counter was propped up by many naval flyers. Rego materialized saying, "Come over and meet the boys," taking me to a group of Dutch flyers with Taco and Remmert already in attendance.

"English is our lingua franca in deference to our host country. This is Eddie, Taco's pilot and this is Mollie, Remmert's pilot. We are now the six musketeers, one for all and all for one! How's that for an introduction? It simply demands a toast, Slamat!"

"That's not English, you dope, that's Malay. He can't even say "Proost" in good undiluted Nederlands," said Eddie. And so it went on until the doors to the dining room were opened for our supper.

Our Pilots

We were all the same rank and nearly all of us were born on the Island of Java in what was then the Netherlands East Indies, except Taco and Remmert. Our pilots were out of a group of forty who came from Java, via Australia and got their pilot's training at the Netherlands Military Flying School in Jackson, Mississippi, USA.

When they arrived in Britain in August 1943, they were boarded on the British aircraft-carrier HMS Argus for day and night deck landing training. After that they went to RNAS Hatston, HMS Sparrowhawk on one of the small islands of Scapa Flow. There they underwent training in day and night torpedo attacks with the British Home Fleet. After that, they trained at RNAS Macrihanish on the Scottish Kintyre peninsula on the east coast where they did rocket firing exercises which then were secret. After that they went to RNAS Maydown, of Londonderry in Northern Ireland. In Derry, they went to the school for submarine warfare after which they were considered as fully trained and ready to join with us. They had flown coastal patrols around Ireland to check on the possibility that German U-boats would use Ireland's neutrality by hiding in their coastal bays. They had also checked on fishing boats in case they were German spy craft. Now they were at RNAS Inskip to join their navigators; hopefully a continuing partnership as our work on the ocean expanse demanded close cooperation and accuracy to survive!

RNAS Inskip

RNAS Inskip was an all-round naval warfare training establishment to train aircrews. The task was to foster close working relationships between pilots and their navigators on small weapons platforms such as the Fleet Air Arm operates from aircraft carriers.

We were qualified for our disciplines. Now we had to combine these into warfare team activities. This was explained to us in a classroom by the Commander of RNAS Inskip, Lieutenant. Commander Raines.

He explained that several training squadrons were standing ready for the various exercises in aircraft for which were specially equipped and armed. The aim was not just to drop a torpedo or fire rockets as our pilots had enough practice at this. But for a combined effort where the navigator got his pilot to the target and talked him into the action. The reverse could also happen where the pilot, constantly aware of his surroundings, would warn his navigator who had his head down working on his navigation, watching his radar screen or busy with his radio, of what was happening or what action he was going to take which required plotting or his attention.

Realistic carrier conditions were observed. The pilot would board his plane, start the engine on the instruction from the control tower, while his navigator received the final briefing of things like the weather report, secret identification codes of the day, type of sea patrol to be carried out, the latest naval intelligent reports, type of weapons carried. Morecombe Bay, just east and southeast of the Isle of Man was used to place the targets and if we were lucky, a real submarine would be our target day or night. We were told to watch the Main Notice Board in the Wardroom in to get our daily routine and duties.

Coch is the Welsh word for red. Cochyn is a derivative that turns it into a nickname for a redhead or a ginger cat. The big ginger cat we met when we arrived was called *Cochyn*. The Wren technician who looked after him was from Wales. Cochyn had come from nowhere and decided that RNAS Inskip was for him so Wren

Megan Evans adopted him. Megan was a real Taff, a nickname for a Welsh person, who worked in the Torpedo workshop as an armorer. Cochyn had his basket and feeding bowl which he called his home. Cochyn was friendly with everybody, even the station commander, and an honored guest in the wardroom.

The men working in the hangers and technical workshops called him the ball bearing mousetrap and spoiled him. That cat had brought a homely feeling to the station, a home away from home!

One day there was a terrible accident in the Torpedo workshop. Nobody knew what had happened, but the top brass weren't talking! Megan Evans was badly injured and was moved from the station's sick bay to a big hospital in Blackpool.

A member of the workshop technicians took Cochyn in a wicker cat container to say, "Hello," to Megan. But Megan was too ill to be allowed visitors and died soon after that.

Cochyn looked all over the station for her. He pawed everybody and gave a meow as if to ask where she was. The whole Station was upset as if in a state of mourning. We witnessed a true state of grief over the loss of Megan. She was taken home with due ceremony to her beloved Wales by the Royal Navy.

The Wren technicians in the Torpedo workshop decided that Cochyn's basket and feeding bowl would remain where it was, and they would act as Cochyn's foster mothers.

GlowWorm

World War II submarines preferred to be on the surface rather than submerged, especially in waters controlled or under surveillance by the enemy. When submerged they could only be detected by acoustic underwater equipment known as ASDIC, Anti-Submarine underwater Detection device, or SONAR, Sound Navigation and Ranging, which is like an underwater radar but uses ultrasonic waves instead of microwaves. It is an echo sounder as it detects the returning echo of the transmitted wave.

Being submerged also had the disadvantage foul internal air-supply by the diesel engine and by the human bodies, and the reduction of the available oxygen to dangerous low levels. This is why they submerged at day time if forced by circumstances and surfaced at night. Being on the surface had the advantage of being capable of higher speeds and at night they were difficult to spot.

The restless, often choppy, wild and noisy North Atlantic Ocean diminished their hearing, so they had to increase lookouts on an already small and overcrowded conning tower to detect approaching aircraft or ships. At the time, German Uboats were not equipped with any form of radar equipment and British radar was at its early stages of development. Even airborne radar equipment was bulky and was treated as a state secret. The German U-boats had heavy machineguns and a small caliber gun and had to be treated with respect and circumspection.

The Swordfish aircraft, although an antiquated biplane, had a desired low speed and reliability for the anti-submarine warfare in the rough North Atlantic Ocean. It was also strong enough as an all-weather plane to withstand rough landing conditions on heaving, rolling flight decks of aircraft carriers. They could carry a torpedo and had the power of a destroyer's broadside with eight rockets. They could sink a submarine with depth charges. Like all weapon systems, they are only as good as the crew that handles them.

Submarine commanders had a great respect for oncoming aircraft and would nearly always crash dive to get under water to try and escape. The most advantageous time to seek, find and sink a German U-boat was if you could use cloud cover or at night and then only with the greatest circumspection. This is where GlowWorm came into play in a night attack.

GlowWorm required the use of the state-of-the-art airborne radar equipment. It had the plan position radar screen with a rotating radar beam showing everything around a three hundred sixty degree sweep as fluorescent blips on the screen. This required a bulky rotating disk-type aerial with supports and motor mechanism. There was no room for this in the body of the Swordfish, so it was under slung in a plastic radome below the engine cowling and attached to the inner starboard wing between the landing wheel mountings. It required the composite newly constructed Mark III to carry it.

Our training Swordfish Mark III was equipped with eight rockets, four under each wing, each rocket head was twenty-five pounds. These solid steel heads were fired at a range of six hundred yards. They would penetrate both the near and far plating of a U-boat pressure hull and then ricochet around inside. The exceptions were the two outer rockets which had specially constructed war heads that were parachute flares named GlowWorm. At that time, these planes, with their secret equipment, were kept in a hangars, guarded day and night, by Royal Marines/ We needed special clearance from our commander to board them. All was set for our first GlowWorm night practice. We took off after sundown on a moonless night. Our target area was in Morecombe Bay where in a place unknown to us was our dummy U-boat target buoy awaiting destruction by rocket fire. On the coast, two observation towers manned by Wrens, took bearings of the fall-of-shot so we could know of our mistakes or success.

In wartime there is no light visible on the ground. All is dark except the starry sky if you're lucky. But our eyes soon grew used to this gloomy darkness. Only the coastline and rivers stood out clearly. The weather was good with little wind and we were warned that when the water was oily or mirror like, due to lack of wind and ripples on the water, it was difficult to judge where air and water met from a moving aircraft. If that was the case, we should abort the exercise. Fresh in everyone's mind was the plane that plunged headlong into the sea killing the crew not long ago.

I told Rego to fly due north two thousand feet hoping to cross the coast which would be clearly recognizable from the air. It also was made easy as the A6 dual carriageway to the north was vaguely visible on our starboard side. It could act as a guide and I told Rego to look for it. We flew until we passed over the coast and I noticed a small blip on my radar screen at about 11 o'clock (note: twelve o'clock is straight ahead, thus this blip was in front of us on our port side). We flew on for a while until my blip on the radar screen moved to the nine o'clock position. In real terms, this blip had not moved. We had moved more to the north. I told Rego to change course to due west "Now!" When on course due west, I talked Rego to the target with my face down watching my radar screen saying, "left, left," or "right, right," or "straight," towards my blip. As we came near I said, "Shallow dive," and when we came near to the target, I said, "now, now, tally ho."

It was now up to Rego. Rego reacted straight away by coming closer to the water and he cried, "Up, up, take care," and he pulled the plane up steeply and let go his two GlowWorms. They fired and swished up in front of us with a trail of flames, then went dead releasing the two parachuted flares. When they illuminated the night with a strong light on the other side of our target as Rego was diving the plane to the silhouetted target with his thumb on the firing button on his joystick.

Just seconds away before letting the steel rockets fly we saw the target was a small fisherman's row boat moored to the target buoy. Rego opened up the throttle, turned, and climbed away into the night.

"Wow, oh Wow, that was close!"

In our headphones we heard a female voice, "Hallo Glow, this is GlowWorm that was a near miss. Return to base and have a drink on us, over and out."

The next morning at breakfast, the commander flew passed our table and said, "Morning boys, had an interesting night, I hear. We'll sort it out with the harbor authorities! Enjoy your breakfast."

"Thank you, sir." we mumbled. That was GlowWorm. Nothing to it, if you say it quickly enough. It nearly sorted out that fisherman! He must have had the fright of his life! We had many more nights of this, without fishing boats, until we were conversant with this tactical procedure.

Combined Attack

If a German U-boat commander stayed on the surface during the day and his U-boat was spotted by an aircraft in midocean, you could bet your bottom dollar he would defend his U-boat with all the armament at his disposal which was to the intruder's peril!

If a Swordfish on patrol from an aircraft carrier away from his convoy detected a submarine on the surface in daytime, good for him. A U-boat's profile is small and the blip on the radar screen is also small. The crew would confirm with each other and the navigator observer would guide his pilot to it until the pilot said, "She's mine." Then the navigator would leave everything to the pilot and update his chart to plot the deviation from his patrol course.

He worked out the U-boat's position in relation to his carrier and would radio transmit the bearing and distance to his carrier. The carrier in turn would signal this information by Aldislamp or searchlight to the Commodore of the Convoy.

Ships at sea in wartime keep radio silence. They communicated by signal lamp. The carrier would then scramble two planes that were standing by, fully armed and fueled for such an eventuality.

The pilot would circle the U-boat outside the range of the U-boat's guns. The U-boat is now in the predicament as a crash-dive would be his probable demise as calling his gunners from their guns to climb up to the conning tower and down into the hull followed by the commander would leave them vulnerable to a full, devastating Swordfish attack before they could dive. It was a cat-and-mouse situation as the Swordfish patiently circled the U-boat until reinforcements arrived. The only escape this U-boat could hope for was that that Swordfish was low on fuel and had to return to base or that it made a suicidal attack on its own and could be shot down.

When the two reinforcement planes arrived, Rego the pilot of the plane who discovered and reported a sub, took command of a combined attack with the three planes one hundred and twenty degrees apart in a circle. The plane carrying a depth charge went in last. Rego and the other plane used their eight rockets first and second. All three acted in quick succession.

Rego gave the radio message, "Now, now, tally-ho," and dived full speed with open throttle towards the U-boat, followed in quick succession by the second plane and then the third. All three flew towards the same target trying not to crash into each other while firing their weapons, then pulling sharply back to their section of the circle. They awaited further instructions. The U-boat could have shot down one of us with luck. With a badly timed attack it could have downed all three of us.

Those are the chances in a war. As the Frenchman say, "C'est la guerre!" It was incumbent on us to exercise this tricky combined attack over and over again. We did this over the Irish Sea by dropping a smoke float and called for backup. In our eagerness, we came very close to each other at times. But we enjoyed the sensual excitement. We also had an instructor flying above us who kept a close eye on us.

At times we heard his voice in our headphones saying. "Well done," or "Are you crazy?"

Black Widow

"The time has come, the walrus said, to talk of many things." There was a time in 1944 when Rego and I were minding our own business, peacefully flying at two thousand feet over the Irish Sea to do something, I forget what, when we noticed a black sleek monoplane flying next to us. It had the American identity star in a roundel on its side and its flaps and wheels were down trying to reduce their speed to match ours.

It had a double cockpit with the flyer at the back cockpit taking pictures of us and both of them waving at us. We waved back and gave them the thumbs-up sign which we hoped would not be construed adversely. Up came their wheels into the body of the plane, up went the flaps and off they peeled with a hell of a lick.

Well now, what do you make of that? Commander Flying told us that an American squadron, with their latest planes, had arrived on an airfield near Liverpool. He thought that the one we saw was a Black Widow. Probably a night fighter with its black livery and that their flyers had thought that we had come out of the ark with our antiquated Swordfish going out to shoot arrows.

We thought that would be that, but we underestimated the Yanks. Three days later coming into the bar before our dinner, we noticed our Commander Flying, the title of a person in command of all flying, entertaining two American officers. He called us over and introduced us to them and said, "These are our six Dutchmen. You met these two before in the air."

From then on, we became the close buddies. The six of us were invited to their wardroom and they would send transport to get us to their airfield and back. All I remember of our visit was the cordial reception we had. The Americans were dry, that is, they did not allow any alcoholic drink on their ships, army camps or airfields. But they had everything else. You name it and they had it: ice cream, cigarettes, chocolates, sweets, and more. And as much as you liked. In wartime that was unheard of!

The Brits said: the Yanks were over-paid, over-dressed, over-sexed, and over here. Mothers, lock up your daughters. They gave us a good time. When they heard that some of us had escaped from the Germans and some from the Japanese they gathered around us and asked unending questions and plied us with all sorts of wonderful and delicious foods and drinks. Ice cream came out of my ears and made me an ice cream addict for life!

However, one item we had never heard of or tasted was Coca Cola. They dished this out for us instead of an alcoholic drink. We liked it. They were surprised that we had never heard of it. Shows you that half the world does not know how the other half lives! In war time we were so starved of delicacies that it was a wonder we did not get sick on them. And our friends were delighted to give it to us. We went back to base with food parcels with all sorts of goodies. What a Black Widow that was!

Meteorology

Forecasting the weather depends heavily on detailed factors determining weather conditions such as atmospheric pressure, temperature, humidity, wind, cloud cover and precipitation such as rain, snow, hail and fog, all measured at twelve-hour intervals. It was kept secret unless from coded messages for radio transmission. The weather reports for aircraft flying over the continent into Germany were made up from a variety of messages from aircraft over the continent, deciphered or cracked coded messages from German stations.

The weather reports for aircraft flying over the vast expanses of the North Atlantic Ocean were scanty, as ships at sea were supposed to keep radio silence and only warships were equipped to code their messages.

We were taught to gauge and appraise the weather conditions we were flying into and were trained to recognize cloud formations, weather fronts, sea conditions, wind findings, and which conditions predicted danger when we were supposed to return to base.

Our Eight Hundred and Sixty Squadron had already lost one Swordfish and its crew. They were on a patrol behind the convoy looking for straggling ships that were missing at daybreak. When they reached their Point of No Return, they discovered that the wind velocity had suddenly changed for the worse and on their return flight to base battled a strong head wind that reduced their ground speed to nearly nil while the convoy moved away from them. They never made it back to base and were never found!

They flew until their fuel ran out. Just before the pilot ditched his plane, the navigator jammed his Morse key down permanently to transmit one long continuous radio signal. The land-based Direction Finder Stations and ships could determine, by taking cross-bearings, where they ditched. If any warships or other ships were near they would have tried to find them.

In the middle of the North Atlantic, at that time of the year, with the sea temperature nearly zero degrees, they would have lasted two to five minutes unless they could have scrambled into the dingy which would have popped out of the wing as soon as the plane landed in the ocean.

No ship in a convoy would stop and leave its convoy and the Royal Naval Destroyer Screen or the aircraft carriers would stay at their post. Their mates on board their carrier did hear them on the radio until they ditched!

Windup

Our training time was nearly over. It was intense, especially for us in a foreign language. But we coped. It was exciting and demanded our full commitment. The final bits consisted of subjects such as: How to communicate with merchant ships from the air and guide stragglers back to the convoy; Search Techniques; Identity Codes and other minor subjects.

We did roughly three hundred and fifty day and forty-five night-hours of flying time. All we had left to do was four days on HMS Argus, an old aircraft carrier, mainly used for training day and night deck landings and some gun firing. For this, we went back to our own Eight Hundred and Sixty Squadron based at RNAS Maydown in Northern Ireland to pick up three Swordfish aircraft.

We were then regarded as fully trained to do First Line duties. We were expected to be: Flying Angels and Killing Devils and at the same time be Officers and Gentlemen! Impossible? We tried it and it was not all that difficult!

As a last farewell to RNAS Inskip and our haunts in Blackpool, we decided to have a night out at the Blackpool Tower Ball Room with its sprung dance floor where Reginald Dixon came out of the stage floor seated in front of his cinema organ playing his signature tune: *I do like to be beside the sea side* with everybody in the Ball Room singing their hearts out!

There was an excited atmosphere when we entered this huge ballroom with its three balconies and we were told that a famous Army Band would play.

We decided to find a seat on the side, get our drinks and watch the American Army chaps carry their instruments on the stage and make all sorts of funny noises tuning their instruments and rattling the drums. Lots of American Army types came, all looking like officers in their well-shaped, smart uniforms, much to the delight of the girls! It was a big band with lots of trombones, clarinets, saxophones and trumpets. Eventually one of the band members placed a notice board in front of the band that said: "The Glen Miller

Army Airforce Band," which was received with great applause. Onto the stage came a good looking American officer carrying a trombone and all the members of the band stood up.

As he reached center stage he turned to face his audience and said, "Hi, my name is Glenn Miller, I hope you will enjoy my music." He turned to face his band, placed the trombone to his lips, tapped his shoe three times and the band started playing *In the Mood* as his signature-tune.

We liked his style of dance band music, especially the swinging rhythm which brought all the American servicemen to the floor with their dancing partners and started swinging and dancing the jitterbug which was new to us.

We tried to imitate the steps and were soon joined by some Wrens who had wanted to teach us. We soon got the hang of it. In particular, we enjoyed his *Moonlight Sonata*, which apparently was an old American tune sung by children for centuries in the southwest of the US of A. It was molded by Glenn into his style of dance band music. This went on until our transport driver reminded us that we should return to base. We had an enjoyable farewell evening!

We counted ourselves lucky to have heard him in reality. He died on December 15, 1944, in a single engine C64 Norseman aircraft travelling to Paris. His body was never found.

The next morning, we went by naval transport to the port of Stranraer, in Scotland, to take the ferryboat to Larne, just north of Belfast in Northern Ireland. There a Royal Netherlands Naval transport picked us up to go across Northern Ireland to RNAS Maydown, just north of Londonderry. The locals call this town Derry.

RNAS Maydown was where our Eight Hundred and Sixty Squadron was based. We arrived on September 16, 1944.

PART 9—MAYDOWN

"Though they go mad they shall be sane, though they sink through the sea they shall rise again; Though lovers be lost love shall not. And death shall have no dominion." Dilon Thomas

Eight Hundred and Sixty Squadron

Eight Hundred and Sixty Squadron of the Naval Air Service of the Netherlands Fleet Air Arm was formed on June 15, 1943, at Donibristle in the County of Fife, Scotland by its first Commander: Lieutenant Commander Pilot Observer RNR Naval Aviation.

Eight Hundred and Sixty Squadron was presently stationed at its home base RNAS Maydown, HMS Shrike on the coast of Lough Foyle in the North East of Ireland, North of Londonderry. This squadron was made up of three flights; O, S, and T, of three or four Swordfish each. They operated from two Merchant Aircraft Carriers. the MAC Macoma and the MAC Gadila and a British MAC ship.

Maydown was part of the British national defenses during World War II, together with two other Air Stations: Ballykelly and Eglington. All three were located near and around Londonderry. They were primarily used to provide shipping and convoy air cover for the North Atlantic region. Maydown was also the home base for Eight Hundred and Thirty-Six Squadron, the largest squadron in the British Royal Navy. It was made up of twenty-three flights of three or four Swordfish each. They operate from seventeen MAC ships; six grain ships and eleven tankers. MAC ships were existing Merchant Navy ships converted with a flight deck. They were slightly shorter and much narrower than the usual Escort Carriers.

They were only able to make twelve to thirteen knots at top speed compared with the Escort Carriers' eighteen knots. This made take-offs somewhat risky in low winds.

Note: For take-offs and landings an aircraft carrier turns into the wind to get the wind to flow from the bow to the stern. They sail into the wind as long as aircraft are landing over the stern or taking off over the bow. This may mean that, in order to avoid a collision with other ships in the convoy, the aircraft carrier cannot stay in the convoy. It may request the Commodore of the Convoy to get a destroyer from the security screen to come to her protection against

German Uboats; if a destroyer can be released from its station around the convoy at the time.

Normally there were two MAC ships to one convoy stationed at the rear of the convoy in an area normally taken up by four merchant ships. They were able to provide six to eight Swordfish for air cover and patrol duties. MAC ships carried almost full cargoes as well as the aircraft, which made the tanker type a floating bomb with oil in her tanks, aircraft fuel, ordnance and weapons. If torpedoed it would blow up sky high!

They were Merchant Navy vessels with Merchant Navy Captains and crews. The aircraft deck handling and flying side of things was carried out by Fleet Air Arm RN personnel. This demanded close liaison between the two types of navy. In reality it was between the Commander Flying and the MAC ship's captain which worked very well!

This was different with the British Royal Navy. They made their officers and men sign on as supernumery Merchant Naval personnel for the duration of the voyage for legal reasons. It could make them pirates or privateers if Royal Navy personnel were serving on a Merchant Navy ship.

To appreciate and understand the British Royal Naval temperament and their characteristic nature, I suggest you approach this subject by telling my Netherlands and American family and friends of the existence of the four different flags or ensigns in British nautical use. Most other countries only have one. All four flags are based on the original English National flag: a white field with a vertical red bar and a horizontal red bar crossing each other in the center of this white field forming the historical St. George Cross. (St. George was depicted on old coins and paintings as a knight in shining armor slaying a dragon.) The Royal Navy carried the White Ensign since early 1600. It was also used as their Battle Ensign; hoisted to the highest masthead to indicate their identity and her battle-ready state to the enemy.

Note: The White Ensign is used in the Royal Yacht Squadron, as well.

The Merchant Navy carried the Red Ensign; a red field with the St. George Cross and although both Navy's were on friendly terms, a large class distinction existed between them. The Royal Navy was the arrogant superior with their greater speed and better armed and equipped ships.

When meeting each other at sea, the Merchant Navy ship first lowered her stern flag in salute. This was then acknowledged by the Royal Navy ship by lowering her stern flag in reply.

From those historical times of pirating and marauding, of sailing ships and man-to-man sea-battles that Merchant ships, officered by Royal Navy officers, were regarded as pirates or privateers. (A privateer was a pirate, licensed, armed and equipped by the British government for a specific political purpose. Where a captured pirate was hanged from the highest yardarm, a privateer had to show his license to save his neck and be released.)

In more recent times, the Royal Navy introduced the Reservist, RNR and the Voluntary Reservist, RNVR officer ranks. In World War II, they had acting or temporary officers. Thus, an officer could be a Lieutenant RNVR Temporarily Acting. Royal Navy ships commanded by an RNR or RNVR officer would carry the Blue Ensign which had a blue field with the St. George Cross.

When Scotland and Wales united with England to form the United Kingdom in 1801, a small flag known as the Union Jack was introduced and flown as the Jack on the bow of naval ships. It was placed in the top quadrant nearest to the flagstaff of the White, Blue and Red Ensigns.

In 1848 it became the National Ensign or flag and could be any size and used by anyone at any time.

Eight Hundred and Sixty Squadron at RNAS Maydown acted as a kind of commissariat service to supply whatever was necessary to keep the flying activities of the three flights for the two Dutch MAC ships in fighting trim. On our arrival, we were told that we were destined to embark upon the MAC Macoma by landing on her in the North Channel between Northern Ireland and Scotland. The rest of the convoy would sail from the Firth of Clyde, make a starboard turn into the North Channel and then into the Atlantic Ocean where they would assemble into their allotted position of a vast convoy of thirty to forty merchant ships on their way to Halifax, Nova Scotia, Canada.

The actual dates were still tentative as it depended on many things. In the meantime, we would attend the Anti Uboat School in Londonderry and carry out Anti U-boat patrols around Ireland.

Note: Ireland was neutral in name. The Allies took that with a grain of salt.

Atlantic Convoys

Within five minutes of Prime Minister Chamberlain announcing that Britain was at war with Germany, the following radio signal went out from Wilhelmshaven to the U-boat fleet: 1105/3/9/39 From Naval High Command-stop To Commanders in Chief and Commanders Afloat-stop Britain and France have declared war on Germany- stop Battle Stations immediately in accordance with Battle Instructions for the Navy already promulgated-out.

That evening the passenger ship Athenia was torpedoed without warning some two hundred and fifty miles northwest of Ireland. By October 16, 1939, 4,205 tons of British merchant ships were sunk. That is approximately one ship for every day of the war. Ships were hastily equipped with one, World War I vintage four-inch gun mounted on the stern and light machineguns of all sorts for use against aircraft such as; the Hotchkiss .303, the Marlin .303, and the Vickers .303. These were manned by a newly formed Defensively Equipped Merchant Ships gunners, from either the Royal Navy or from the Maritime Anti-Aircraft Regiment who were hastily trained in handling these guns.

The bridge and the wheelhouse were shielded with concrete armor against bullets and flying shrapnel as U-boat gunners made it a habit to shoot at the bridge and wheelhouse.

Ships under a U-boat attack send out an S S S signal. Ships under aircraft attack sent out an A A A signal. The Focke Wulf FW200 Condor was a German long-range aircraft, with 3.530 km range, that spotted for the U-boats. Fighters were dispatched to shoot them down if they were within range.

In general terms, the Anti- Submarine Warfare suffered from a lack of equipment. It was slowly being improved with assistance from Lend-Lease from the U.S. In the beginning, there was also a lack of training, training facilities, information and technology.

The greatest strains of the war at sea fell on the shoulders of the masters or captains and mates or desk officers. Their ships were slow and maneuvered like the lumbering barges they were. Station keeping in convoy was an unending ordeal. Ships were positioned five hundred yards apart on either side and one thousand yards fore and aft. Convoys had a typical escort of seven destroyers, nine corvettes, and three frigates plus two MAC ships who also had the duty of refueling the frigates in mid Atlantic. On a dark, moonless night it required nerves of steel and the eyes of a cat to keep station properly within ones allotted position in the convoy. Vigilance could never be relaxed!

In poor visibility on a foggy night or stormy weather, it was impossible and created stragglers. They veered and straggled and became easy targets for stalking U-boats. The men in the engine room suffered the tortures of the damned. They never knew when a torpedo might tear through the thin plates of the hull, sending their ship plunging to the bottom before they could reach the first rung of the ladder to the deck. Burdened, as they often were, with bulk cargoes, ships sank like punctured tin cans filled with lead shot.

When a ship was torpedoed, it fell back and slowly sank, ablaze in flames if it was a tanker. The space left was closed up immediately and ships who were companions of many days sailed on without stopping. For those who took to lifeboats or rafts, the process of dying was prolonged. At war's end in August 1945, twenty-nine thousand and eighty British and six thousand three hundred Dutch merchant seamen had lost their lives in the conflict. Almost half of them were on tramp ships and others were tragically in lifeboats and on rafts. The maximum time seamen were on a life raft before they were rescued was three months.

The dividing line between tramp and cargo liner was very thin at times. But in general, the average World War II tramp was about five thousand tons gross, blunt in the bow, rounded in the stern and capable of carrying a vast amount of bulk or general cargo. She boasted a forest of spindly derricks and winches and had tall masts.

Accommodation for her crew was often an afterthought in a dark, airless cavern under the forecastle head, sleeping in two-tiered bunks that rose and fell like high-speed lifts with every swell that passed under the bow.

Tramps normally went all over the world, wherever their owners had made a transport deal. Cargo liners had a regular itinerary, engaged in the cross trades.

Battle of the Atlantic

"The Battle of the Atlantic was a dominating factor all through the war. We could never forget that everything happening elsewhere, on land, at sea, or in the air, depended ultimately on its outcome and amid all other cares we viewed its changing fortunes day by day with hope or apprehension."—Winston Churchill

Tales of hard and unremitting toil, often under conditions of acute discomfort and frustration and always in the presence of unseen danger was lighted by incident and drama. For the individual sailor or airman there were few moments of exhilarating action to break the monotony of an endless succession of anxious, uneventful days. Dire crisis might flash on the scene with brilliant fortune or glare with mortal tragedy at any moment.

Many gallant actions and incredible feats of endurance were recorded, but the deeds of those who perished will never be known.

A sketch of what happened in the following scenario in early 1943 is vast and nearly beyond comprehension. It starts with the U-boats in France, who normally concentrated their attacks on The Gap in the mid-Atlantic, where slow moving convoys were not protected by air patrols operating from Canada, Greenland or Oban in Scotland. Once German Admiral Donitz got a sniff of a convoy, he organized his Uboats in line abreast across the route he expected it to take.

Twelve U-boats, maybe twenty miles apart, in possibly two or even three lines deep with twelve miles between lines added up to twenty-four to thirty-six U-boats or more. They stayed near stationary on the surface and waited for the convoy to steam into them. The distance from New York or Halifax to this unprotected Gap in the Atlantic is approximately eight hundred miles. It took two to three days to reach the U-boat hunting line due to slow convoy speeds. The U-boats were on battle stations, alert and keeping radio silence until one of the U-boats sighted the convoy. Then they gave a short signal, a two to eight letter code, giving position, course and speed of the convoy. The Germans divided the

Atlantic in numbered grids. Thus, U-boats used this grid system which greatly reduced the message length. More importantly, it reduced the ability of detection by the convoys' direction-finding equipment. It then followed the convoy at a safe distance sending contact signals every two hours. The other U-boats on receiving these messages would converge on that moving location and warn other U-boats who may not have received these messages. They drew in as many U-boats as possible. They waited until darkness; their preferred time to attack! The adverts and commercial radio messages in Britain and America that said, "Careless lips cost ships," probably leaked like a sieve!

The Atlantic covers approximately thirty-two million square miles. That's a lot of ocean and the convoy did not have the slightest idea where and what was awaiting them! To complicate this sketch still further, there were three convoys leaving the United States as follows:

Convoy SC122 departed from New York at a speed of seven knots. The speed of a convoy is the speed of the slowest ship in that convoy. It carried fuel oil, iron ore, steel, wheat, bauxite, sugar, refrigerated meat, zinc, tobacco, and army tanks in fifty merchant ships.

Convoy HX229 departed from New York at a speed of ten knots, three days later, carrying explosives, lubricating oil, refrigerated dairy products, manganese, lead, timber, phosphate, diesel oil, aviation fuel, sugar and powdered milk; two weeks supply of powdered milk for the entire British Isles, in forty merchant ships.

Convoy Hx229A departed from New York at a speed of eleven knots, one day later, carrying similar cargoes as the other two in twenty-seven merchant ships.

They had a gross registered tonnage of just under one million tons plus cargo of another million tons. They carried nine thousand merchant seamen and one thousand passengers; mainly service men, some ladies from the American Red Cross and a party of

Catholic missionaries. All this steamed towards forty-six U-boats, one thousand miles from land. A nightmare scenario!

U-boats preferred to attack at night as that allowed them to operate faster on the surface and fires from ships that were hit illuminate other targets. A U-boat's surface range at that time was sixty-five thousand miles. They had all slipped their moorings at the French port of Saint Nazaire and slipped out at night through the Bay of Biscay. They were managed from their headquarters at the Bois de Boulonge in Paris.

When the attack started there was utter panic. Convoys zigzagged, made emergency turns which were difficult maneuvers with forty some ships. The three convoys battled for a week until they reached British air-cover. By then they had lost twenty-two merchant ships, one hundred and fifty thousand tons of Allied shipping was destroyed, one hundred and sixty thousand tons of cargo was lost including a two-week supply of powdered milk, and about four hundred were dead; mostly Americans. Only one U-boat was sunk. For a time, it looked as if this battle might have reached the Desired Sinking Rate.

The Desired Sinking Rate was an average of seven hundred thousand tons of shipping sunk per month per year for Britain to starve into submission. This rate was calculated by the German Commander-in-Chief, Grand Admiral Raeder. As it happened, it was not far off, but was not reached yet. It was also the turning point in ships lost due to increased improved technology like ASDIC, Hedgehog mortars and surface radar and an increase in naval escorts. Even so, 1,667 merchant ships were lost against 87 U-boats.

Mac "Macoma"

October 26, 1944, RNAS Maydown, HMS Shrike, Section Eight Hundred and Sixty Squadron was a busy place from early in the morning. Ground crew and technicians were preparing our four new Fairey Swordfish Mark III aircraft fitted with the latest state-of-the-art equipment—the latest radar, rockets, and fine-pitched propellers driven by 690 pk Bristol Pegasus motors. Preparations were for our first flight on the MAC Macoma where they were waiting for us to land as they were coming down the Firth of Clyde. Scotland to join our allotted convoy bound for Halifax, Nova Scotia, Canada.

Our luggage was already stowed into the empty air gunner's cockpit. With all that extra equipment, air gunners were not carried anymore. If any gun shooting was done, the observer/navigator had to do it. While all this went on, we struggled into our flying kit and checked each other to make sure we had everything. The four pilots stumbled out to a van with parachutes bouncing against the back of their legs, to be taken to their aircraft. The four observers/navigators carrying their parachutes, plotting tables, and binoculars had their own van take them to the briefing room in the control tower to receive the final instructions, information and identity cartridges for a fary pistol.

I climbed up the side of my Swordfish into my cockpit assisted by ground staff who also handed up the plotting table, parachute and binoculars. I settled down, clipped my parachute into position, hooked the binoculars into its nook and plugged the jack of my headphones into the intercom plug. I said, "Hi, I'm in. Give me some time to sort things out."

"Took you some time. Hurry, the weather seems to be changing," Rego replied.

I took the plotting table out of its canvas bag and clipped it into its place, organized my pencils and eraser on a string round my neck, strapped my navigational computer on my right upper leg, and heard, "Don't forget your monkey strap," over the intercom.

↑ Taking off   and   Landing ↓

"Thanks, Rego."

I did just that before I checked my watch, switched on the radio and called the control tower:

"Hallo Fish, this is Fish two, ready for takeoff, over."

"Thank you, Fish two, just hang on and wait for your green."

On the intercom: "Please keep an eye on the tower, I still have something to do."

"Okay."

The radio came on. "All Fishes, this is Fish control. Weather is deteriorating from the north. Proceed overland to Red Bay or Garron Point and then to your destination. Confirm reception, Fish one, over."

"This is Fish one, received and understood, over and out."

"This is Fish two, received and understood, over and out." And so it went.

We soon saw the green light from the control tower, waited for Fish one to taxi to the starting point, followed her and the other two followed us. Being a grass-carpeted airfield, we took off in two's and were soon at two thousand feet followed by the other two.

We did not fly close in formation as it was tiring for the pilots. We could still see clearly and saw the coastline on our left until we reached Red Bay and Garron Point. Turning northeast we saw MAC Macoma way out in the distance coming down the Clyde.

Intercom: "Are you sure that's her?"

My reply: "What have you got in your eyes?" My binoculars put me in a superior position, so I replied, "Sure I'm sure. Just follow Fish one. He's sailed on her before and must recognize her."

Soon enough we heard the radio from Fish one make contact with our carrier followed by, "All Fishes, this is Fish one, stand by to land."

We all started flying in line astern while the carrier corrected its course into the wind.

I secured all my bits and pieces and was ready, facing forward and bracing myself for a heavy landing but looking forward over the port side out of pure curiosity (which killed the cat). It was soon our turn and Rego made a nice landing. It was abruptly stopped by one of the arrestor wires. Then we were pushed by the deck handling crew to join Fish one on the other side of the crash barrier. Fish three and four soon followed. Nice to land on the comparatively smooth waters of a Scottish Loch. The crash barrier came down and we climbed down from our cockpits assisted by deck handling crewmen who smiled and said, "Welcome on board, Sir. Please leave your gear in your cockpit; you may need them soon. We'll cover the cockpits against the rain. Your luggage will be taken to your cabin."

"Thank you, sir."

We were lead into the island and requested to take off our parachute harness only. There were special hooks to hang them on. Then we were shown into a little ward room where we were welcomed by our Commander Flying Lieutenant. Commander van Vlaander, "Call me Hans."

He went on, "Gentlemen, you are most welcome on board but please do not take off your flying clothes as we are now under the Convoy commodore's orders who may need you at any time from now on until the convoy has been put in order. Please wash your hands and face, if you wish, have a cup of soup, coffee or tea with a sandwich, but remain on stand-by."

All this was in Dutch, a nice surprise. We sat down, relaxed and were served by a smiling steward.

We were shown to our tiny cabin; two bunks on either side; no portholes; everything around us was steel with two small floor mats by each bunk, reading lamps screwed to the steel wall at each bunk head and a steel clothes locker at each bunk end. The ablution facilities were at the end of the passage and small; just big enough to serve two persons. Home-from-home!

Eventually, a message came from the commodore's destroyer, "Flights S and F stand down."

Our Commander Flying decided that S flight would be on white alert until the following morning at 08:00. That which meant; fully dressed with flying underwear but no flying over wear. Blue alert meant fully dressed for flying with flying helmet, parachute and harness at the ready. Red alert meant fully dressed, ready for flying at any moment's notice, sitting in the briefing room, at night in red light to accustom your eyes to darkness.

At night, we were guided to our aircraft by a deck handler, so we did not walk into a rotating propeller!

We were lucky that the carrier could take us aboard with a southwesterly breeze as the Clyde was not broad enough to allow this with a northerly wind. Although the bad weather was coming from the north, based on the weather pattern, RNAS Maydown had foreseen this and wisely sent us to Red Bay.

A crash barrier is like a tennis net made of steel cables. It lies flat on deck between steel posts and comes up under steam pressure when needed. We hope we would never need it as it is the last safety barrier when a plane's landing hook misses the four arrester wires and flies into the barrier with catastrophic results. It breaks or bends the propeller out of all recognition, damages the motor and its cowling and breaks all sorts of other things. Hopefully it does not harm the crew.

Arrester wires are steel cables lying flat on deck. Each end goes down to hydraulic brakes. When a plane comes in to land, these arrester wires are raised about twelve centimeters from the deck so that the plane's landing hook below its tail; released by the pilot, hooks onto one of the arrester wires. The plane then comes to an abrupt stop. The hydraulic brakes bring it from landing speed of seventy to eighty kilometers to a standstill in ten to fifteen meters.

The difference between landing a plane on land and landing on the deck of a carrier is that on land the plane comes in low and makes a two-point landing with the tail up on the two front wheels, then slowly lowers the tail to the ground. When making a deck landing one flies onto the deck high in a three-point posture; the front wheels and the tail wheel at the same level, then lower the landing hook under the tail to give this hook the maximum chance to pick up one of the arrestor wires and hope for the best! Coming in high avoids coming too near the rounded stern end of the flight deck. That has a downdraft which can suck the plane down with disastrous consequences. This is why pilots and batsmen are well trained!

When you drive a car towards a manhole cover in the road, the metal cover disappears under the bonnet before you reach the cover. The same happens to a ship's stern when you fly low towards a ship from the back. The ship's stern, then the ship itself will disappear under the propeller and the engine cowling. The pilot needs all the help he can get if he wants to land safely. This was done by the Batsman. That was in my time—nowadays it is done by the wizardry of mirrors, lights and electronics. The Batsman was a specially trained pilot. He had two white round tennis rackets which he kept in outstretched arms and had a big white dot on his chest. When all three white dots are in line, it means steady as you go. When the left arm goes down and the right arm up, it means your starboard wing is too low. When he circles his right-hand bat high above his head, it means abort, try again.

With a string of Bat signals he tells the pilot how his position is in relation to the deck he wants to land on. The pilot and the Batsman want to land the plane to catch one of the arrester wires which is roughly in the center of the ship. Take off the length of the Swordfish and the tail with its landing hook is roughly where it should hook one of these wires. If the Batsman judges the plane is right to land, he gives the cut engine signal; bats crossed below the knees. In the beginning of the pilot's training, this is quite an anxious moment. He is still airborne but, he has to instantly obey all Batsman signals.

North Atlantic

The North Atlantic Ocean is an extremely large area of water. It stretches roughly from Ireland and France on the east to America and Canada on the west and from Greenland on the north to the Azores in the south.

The North Atlantic has extreme weather conditions. As we are entering this area in mid-autumn we expect the harsh winter conditions to start with stormy and icy moods.

The vastness of this area is expressed and measured in spherical measurements which are not very well understood by my family and friends who are stern and uncompromising landlubbers. At the price of being called pedantic, I will make this explanation as lenient as I know how!

The last landmark of Britain we saw was the Mull Of Kintyre, Scotland. It is on the world sphere at approximately fifty-five degrees north of the Equator and nearly six degrees west of the zero meridian of Greenwich. To put this in context, fifty-five degrees north of the Equator in the Americas is Labrador, Canada.

Our convoy had to go to Halifax, Nova Scotia, Canada. It is at approximately forty-four degrees north of the Equator and sixty-five degrees west of the zero meridian of Greenwich. To put this in context with Europe, that would place Halifax at the Southern French Mediterranean coast.

Thus, we had to go south eleven degrees and across the North Atlantic fifty-nine degrees west. It took us thirty-five days with a slow convoy, some atrocious weather and many course changes by command of the Convoy commodore.

We were in the North Atlantic and could feel the difference between the swell we had in the Scottish lochs and the long heaving swells of the ocean. The weather was overcast with a rising chilly wind strength and with a view that was still clear with a well-defined horizon. We saw our British sister MAC ship the MAC Mahon, another tanker with four Swordfish on her flight deck. Then we saw some destroyers and frigates scurrying around, shepherding the convoy into shape. From where we were it all looked very well organized, but you have to be in the air to be able to overlook forty to fifty merchant ships and make a judgment. Convoys varied in size; the number of ships could vary from thirty to one hundred and fifty ships. Our convoy had forty-four ships. A signal light flashed calling us from one of the destroyers. The message must have come from the Convoy commodore.

Light signals to our ship were received by a signalman on the bridge, but the observers/navigators on our flight deck, watching these goings on, read the message as saying, "MAC Macoma from Commodore stop welcome to our menagerie stop frigate twenty-seven will show you to your position stop wishing you Godspeed."

Frigate twenty-seven came alongside and shot a line across to us which had a message cylinder attached to it. It was collected and shot back to her. We all waved, and she veered away to station herself in front of us, leading us to our position at the back of the convoy. We saw her doing the same to our sister MAC ship. We were now ready for our task with the other destroyers and frigates.

The night was setting in. We went to the small wardroom for our drinks, after which we were called for supper. We had one big watertight steel door into the island that got us from the flight deck to our quarters. That steel door had a high threshold to step over and once inside the island we went down a steel flight of stairs to get to our quarters, well below the flight deck.

After supper we were called upstairs to the plotting and briefing rooms, which were on flight deck level in the island below the wheelhouse. The captain's bridge is above that. We settled in the briefing room and relaxed in the easy chairs until Flight Commander Hans, came in to give us the lowdown on the situation we were in.

This was his report: The RAF Costal Command had sent three long range Short Sunderland aircraft on patrol in front of our convoy to search for possible U-boats. The Germans called the Short Sunderland "eine fliegende stachelschwein" a flying porcupine because of its eighteen machine guns sticking out all over its fuselage. It could carry a nine-hundred-kilogram bomb load and depth charges. Recently it received airborne radar and the U-boat commanders respected its killing capabilities. But they could not cover the gap, the Air Gap. That's where we came in.

Latest intelligence of German U-boat activities was that they were severely thrashed with the installation of lightweight airborne radar sets. U-boats were now more easily detected, especially at night which had been their preferred attack time. Although they were equipped with more and better guns and machine guns, they still preferred to crash dive when seeing aircraft. This reduced their speed and killing capabilities. So the aircraft may not see any U-boats but their presence would have a demoralizing, detrimental effect on them. Making them crash dive slowed them down considerably so that the convoy could pass them out of harm's way.

U-boats were now equipped with good underwater acoustic listening devices, such as the ASDIC so they could detect ship noises and an approaching large convoy with ease.

As a convoy approached, their latest tactics were to place themselves in front of the convoy, dive low and lie still to prevent detection by the destroyer screen. They let the convoy move over them and came up to periscope depth in the middle of the convoy to do their killing job.

ASDIC pings were the bursts of acoustic sound that were transmitted to get an echo ping back that bounced off any underwater object. This always gave away the presence of the transmitting station, so it became a Hobson's Choice for the German submariner. A poor choice could turn out to be a deadly one. Many of them regretted being too inquisitive.

We were given our duty roster for dealing with coded messages from western approaches at Liverpool for things like updating charts and maps, latest weather reports, intelligence reports. This work was done in the briefing room. We were still under White Alert but would soon be changed to Blue Alert, unless a Red Alert came over the Tannoy with its "V" in Morse code. It sounded its loud message over and over again to the whole ship. The call to Action Stations gave one a real start!

We were dismissed and went down to the bar in the small wardroom.

Before going to sleep, most of us went for a stroll on the flight deck. We noticed that our Swordfish were all strapped down, with wings folded back between the upright metal weather shields which were part of the flight deck. They normally lay flat on deck.

The weather had deteriorated with a stronger chillier wind, heavy overcast, but no rain and a clear view. We could see our sister MAC ship and some merchant ships around us, like darkened ghost ships. The swells felt a bit longer as we watched the flight deck moving up and down slower than before as the convoy moved into the center of the North Atlantic with its long towering swells. Without our duffle coats on we were cold and went into the island and down to our quarters to prepare for a good night's sleep.

Coming from land, you have to get used to ship's noises, engine tremblings, and the odd squeak, but mainly you have to get used to the ship's movements—the rolling and the heaving. At sea you slept on horsehair mattresses, although they felt solid and hard at first, you got used to them quickly. The bunks were narrow. If the ship started heaving and swaying, you could wedge yourself between the wooden sides which were made like a box. The first night was always the getting used to it night, but I was tired and soon fell asleep.

I had a bad dream and heard the Morse V sign sounding over and over again until Rego shook me awake and shouted, "Red Alarm, Red Alarm, get out. We are S flight and must dress for action. No time to wash, get going!"

Wow! Talk about waking up in a hurry! Luckily, we had laid out all our flying underwear in case some Schweinehund messed with us. I don't know if we broke a record, but we were in all that warm underwear in a jiffy, while the Tannoy screeched out its V signs. We dressed into our battle dress, flying overalls, heavy white long socks, flying boots and ran upstairs into the briefing room where our steel lockers were.

The briefing room was illuminated in red light to accustom our eyes to the outside darkness. We put on the rest of our outfit; fur lined jacket, May West, and parachute harness. Rego and Eddie left us to go on deck to look if their plane was in good order. I gathered my plotting board, strapped on my leg computer and scribbling pad, my binoculars and parachute and collapsed into one of the briefing room chairs.

Oh God, where are my pencils and eraser and compass. Stop panicking!"

They were in my plotting board bag. The Tannoy had stopped screeching and was quiet; it was peaceful! The other observer/navigator, Taco was already seated in his chair and gave me a broad grin and said, "Never a dull moment!"

"I could not agree more."

We sat quietly listening to the ships' noises and could distinctly hear the sound of distant depth charge underwater explosions; a short sharp crack followed by a booming deep resonant sound. There were also bursts of multiple explosions which must have come from the Hedgehog, a multiple piece of ordnance at the forward end of a destroyer. It consisted of twelve mortars, simultaneously throwing a pattern of twelve depth charges forward over the bow, hoping to surround the U-boat with exploding depth charges. The bigger depth charges are thrown off the stern, which is less accurate than the Hedgehog.

The flight commander came in and said, "Morning; there's very little good about it! From the commodore the message says: 'Three destroyers engaging suspect ASDIC signals in front of convoy stop scramble S flight for forward patrols stop keep F flight on standby for possible direct assistance out.'" He went on to say, "It is now 05:25 and still dark but will soon become light. Rego and you will fly from left side of the convoy straight forward for forty miles then do a Viper patrol and return to base."

"The same for S-two, Eddie and Taco, but starting on the right side. This convoy is about three miles wide. Coming back, keep an eye open for the Mahon boys. They are on Blue Alert and may have had to scramble! The convoy is moving towards Greenland, course three hundred degrees, seeking long-range in the gap. I don't know of any convoy course changes planned but you never know! If all goes well, we expect you back in about three hours. Good luck!"

The NCO armourer stepped forward and told us that we would be carrying one depth charge, eight rockets, six smoke floats, two pans of .303 for the rear Vickers and a full belt of .303 for the forward Vickers. He gave each of us six signal cartridges for the identity of this day which I put in my plotting board bag. Taco and I put on all the gear necessary for flight including; our flying helmets, the parachute harness, our flying gloves, our plotting board bag, our parachute and slung our binoculars round our neck. We stumbled to the steel outside door which was opened for us and stepped over the steel threshold into darkness. We heard the two engines ticking over and felt a hand on our shoulders and a voice in the darkness:

"Just put your hand on my shoulder and follow me. You get accustomed to the darkness soon, but do not leave me until I guide you to your Swordfish."

We followed our guide until we stood next to our plane. By now we could distinguish things clearly. I noticed that my Swordfish had her wings in place and was pushed to the middle line facing the bow ready for takeoff. I also noticed that Taco's Swordfish still had her wings folded, waiting for us to takeoff so they could be pushed to the middle line. With the help of my guide, I climbed up and into my cockpit and was handed the rest of my gear.

I switched on my low-level cockpit light, radio, radar and plugged my helmet plug into the intercom plug.

Before I could speak, Rego's voice said, "What kept you so long? I'm frozen."

"Sorry Rego, the baby was crying. Give me a little more time, I've got to sort myself out."

"And don't forget your monkey tail, otherwise you'll never hear that baby cry again."

"Okay, okay."

Crazy dialogue kept us sane, I think.

I settled in, told Rego the details of the briefing when all of a sudden, the deck lights went on. Deck lights were like the cat's eyes on a motorway; unidirectional, only to be seen by oncoming traffic. On the flight deck, they could only be seen from the stern and then only above the horizontal. The green light came from the bridge and Rego opened the throttle wide and the engine roared into full life. We started rolling forward with deck hands holding both wing ends until we went too fast, roared past the island and over the bow into the night.

The plane hung on its prop and slowly climbed into the air. From my cockpit, it was always an exciting sight to see the ship in its fullness disappearing behind us as the plane gained height going for the left side of our convoy which was clearly visible below us as blacked out ghost ships in the night.

We reached the left side of the convoy and I told Rego to fly over the left and foremost ship and set his pilot compass to three hundred degrees or west north west, the course of our convoy for forty miles where we were going into a Viper patrol.

A Viper patrol is a zigzag, where the zigs and zags depend on the visibility which I had to determine, plot and tell Rego the new course as the zig became a zag. To make a long story short, we returned in broad daylight just in time for a lovely breakfast.

We sat subdued eating our breakfast. We had a bad experience and were not in the mood to discuss it further I hoped to forget, but it has always been in my mind!

But what did we see on the flight? The ocean is like a desert of water instead of sand. Looking down you can see white crested waves known as white horses. You can determine the wind direction at sea level, which might or might not be the same as at our height. Then your eyes move towards the horizon, it becomes a grey-green or grey expanse with nothing on it. "How boring! Until a whale blows his nose! It seems endless!"

At that time, if I was not plotting I sat with my face glued to my radar to see nothing interesting, until I cried, "Rego, a good blip at one o'clock. Can you see anything? Steer zero three zero. I plotted it so give a shout if you see something."

"Okay, okay."

Off we went to look. Our job was to investigate and what we found was awful! It was a sea battered lifeboat with five dead persons looking at the sky with hollow eyes which were picked out by seagulls.

They must have drifted for a long time as their flesh was in tatters. We reported its position in relation to our convoy; that is bearing and distance and went on to complete our patrol.

Back far right C. Gutteling

PART 10—BAD WEATHER

Noses are red
My feet are blue
Shiver in my pants
But my aim is true

Transfer of Diesel Oil

We were approaching the twentieth meridian of longitude; roughly the beginning of the Air Gap, at an approximate latitude of fifty-five degrees north. The weather, in North Atlantic terms, was reasonably good. It was overcast with a long heavy ocean swell, a bit breezy but good enough for pumping ship's diesel fuel from our tanks to the frigates escorting our convoy. We were keen to watch this and waited for the commodore to tell our captain to make the necessary preparations.

The activities on the flight deck, early on the next morning, told us below that things were happening. We hurried to get dressed to look at how the oil feeding procedures were handled in mid-Atlantic without changing course or speed. On deck, we were surprised to see that our four Swordfish aircraft were pushed and strapped down in a neat row on the port side to give working space for all the gear required and its handling.

One of the escort frigates was following us at close quarters on the port beam where a long boom could be lowered with a float or small buoy attached to a long line. It could be paid out for as far as necessary. By now, groups of curious onlookers watched every move.

The likely place to fall overboard on most ships is the port side as the suction into the ship's screw is less than on the starboard side. That is if you could jump far enough away from the ship's hull. That was the reason for the long boom. It prevented the float from being sucked in when lowered into the water! Most ship's screws turn clockwise when viewed from the stern. This creates a suction on the starboard side as the screw blades chop down. The hull creates an equal suction on both sides as it moves through the water. All in all, falling overboard is not to be recommended!

To cut this short; following are the major moves to complete a successful transfer of diesel oil.

The boom on the port beam is lowered and the float let down into the water which was quickly taken back towards the frigate. They picked it up by hauling it in with the line.

The line on the frigate was attached to a heavy rope-cable. In the meantime, our end of the float line was handed down to chaps one deck below us. They waited for a sign from the frigate, then they hauled in the line with the heavy cable attached that was paid out from the frigate.

The heavy cable was firmly attached to a large metal reinforced rubber pipe. It had rubber float rings attached to it, approximately one meter apart. By now the frigate had moved to our starboard close quarter. On a sign that she was ready, our boys paid out the rubber pipe which they hauled in with the heavy rope cable.

Once the rubber pipe was coupled to her diesel oil inlet valve and plenty of slack given to the rubber oil pipe which bounced around in the waves, the frigate hoisted a flag. That was the sign for us to start pumping diesel oil. Once she had her fill, the flag came down and we stopped pumping diesel oil. The frigate gave a blare on her siren and sent a light signal message which was, "Burb Burb stop TU." (TU is thank you.) And that was that! Roll on the next frigate.

While all this went on, MAC Mahon was standing by in case of an alarm.

Notions Galore

The weather was the all-consuming topic of the day as was the state of the ocean we were plowing through. The movements of the ship were commensurate with the capers and caprioles of the waves.

After transferring diesel oil to all our frigates in comparatively reasonable conditions, we moved into an area of low depression with deteriorating weather and seas. Our daily patrols became more and more unpleasant; even tricky and dangerous both for the pilot, taking off and landing on a heaving, rolling flight deck and for the navigator, keeping his plot in stormy conditions and wind changes. It was a relief to feel your Swordfish hit the flight deck correctly and feeling the arresting gravitational forces push you forward.

We already had two Swordfish aircraft out of commission with broken under carriages where the landing aircraft came down and met a heaving flight deck coming up fast. The result was a heavy landing, luckily without injuries to the fliers. The poor Batsman stood in wind and rain, strapped to the flight deck, trying to tell the incoming pilot what to do to get safely on board. At times this was an impossible task on a heaving, rolling deck. No wonder he needed a stiff drink when coming off duty!

Our convoy changed course to approach the Canadian coast and make for Halifax. It was still a long ways off.

We entered the Labrador Basin and passed the Grand Banks of Newfoundland. With its constant winter mist and fog conditions, there was for us nothing to look forward to.

We had more patrols to our rear to look for straggling merchant ships. We disliked doing this as we were scared of sudden weather changes that would cut us off from our convoy and MAC ships with fatal consequences.

As it was cold, wet, windy and nasty on the flight deck, we spent most of our time reading or playing Lie and Dice, a card game. It kept us busy for hours on end with lots of laughter and drollery. In fact, it kept us sane and filled the bar kitty for a good meal ashore.

The First Radar on a Merchant Ship

Our flight commander, Hans, a pleasant two-and-a-half ringer, a lieutenant commander pilot, was tall and looked older than the rest of us, but he was still very much one of us. Hans had to make tough decisions at times and also acted as our paterfamilias.

At my request, we sat opposite each other in the otherwise empty briefing room for a friendly pow-wow. He listened attentively to a notion I had for a while. It buzzed in my bonnet and I thought it could be carried out with his approval and assistance.

I pointed out to him that as yet, no merchant ships had any radar and that even larger warships had to share the information from the massive aerial and equipment radar that was installed on some battleships and cruisers. Those ships informed their escorts by light signals if anything important showed up on their radar. Hans probably already knew these things, but he let me waffle on.

I reminded him that we had two Swordfish aircraft out of commission, strapped to the flight deck in front of the crash barrier. They were equipped with the latest state-of -the-art aircraft lightweight radar and even if damaged, could possibly be cannibalized for spare parts and a good radar set made from it.

I asked if I could place the plastic aerial radome on top of the bridge with the radarscope on the captain's bridge with the aid of our radar technicians. And, possibly have another screen in the wheelhouse below the bridge. We make history by being the first merchant ship to carry a plan position with an all-round radar view!

"Is that all?" he dryly remarked with a smile. "I never expected anything like this when you requested a private talk. It sounds a plan worth giving a try, but I have to get the captain on our side. Wait here until I come back."

So I sat quietly reading a technical magazine until the captain and Hans came in for a further pow-wow.

The captain, in his Shell Oil uniform, was an older man with grayish hair, broad and strong looking but with a smiling face. He shook my hand and said, "You've thrown the cat among the pigeons! I think it is a worthwhile plan. Let me know if we can help you with men or material. You may start as soon as you wish with the consent of your flight commander."

I told him that my first problem was to get the same electrical power supply from his ship as we used in our Swordfish. I needed assistance in getting on top of his bridge and help from one of his crew to bolt down the radar radome, with aerial equipment bolted inside, strong enough to withstand storm winds.

"I'll give two of my best chaps, one is our electrician and the other one is a ship's rigger and an all-round handyman. Between the two of them there's very little they can't fix. I'll send them to you and you can tell them what they are in for. Okay?"

Hans agreed and told our radar technicians to report to me. The captain then invited us to his cabin to have a drink and a bite, so we all went down to his cabin just under the bridge, and a good time was had by us!

After breakfast the next morning, I was told that four sailors were waiting for me in the briefing room. I hurried to the room and found all four standing. I put them at ease and told them to relax, asked them to sit down and listen carefully.

"Do you know what you are here for?"

All four said, "No, sir."

I started the same way as I had with the flight commander and ship's captain. I thought they should know the whole plan, so a good job would be done! They listened with growing attention. I told them that the captain, the flight commander, the four of them and myself were the only persons who knew about this plan. The four of you will be the center pieces that could make it work, if possible! I requested that they kept it among themselves until the actual work started.

"I won't have to tell you that this job on top of the bridge can be dangerous as there are no rails. You need to work with a safety harness connected to a lifeline which is connected to the mast or some solid anchorage. Also, I want you to work in pairs so one can assist the other. If you wish more than two can work together. Feel free to ask anything you require, and any suggestions are always welcome.

I'll leave you alone to have your own pow-wow. After that I will be most interested to know if you think it can be done and how and what you require to do it. I'll send you some coffee and please remember keep it to yourselves. Any questions?"

"No; not yet anyway," was their reply so I left the room.

"Oh yes," I said sticking my head round the door, "When the flying alarm sounds, you must leave this room and man your post! I'll see to it that you are not disturbed," and closed the door.

Coming down I met Hans and told him about our meeting. He said he would like to hear their verbal report and that he agreed with the rest. A passing steward was told to bring four coffees and cake to the briefing room and that nobody was to disturb them.

Sometime later, the steward told me that the four in the briefing room were ready to report to me. I told him to tell the flight commander that he was requested in the briefing room.

There we were; six of us counting the flight commander who told me to lead the meeting.

"Who will be your spokesman?"

They pointed to the ship's rigger and he was requested to make their case.

"First requirement, sir, is to get the right power supply. Our electrician says he can rewire a spare transformer he has in his store. With the assistance of one of our radar technicians, they think that it can be done. Secondly, I can get hold of two safety harnesses that we use for painting the ship's hull and enough rope to suit our purpose. Thirdly, I have all the tools required to anchor the radar radome and tie it down with a piece of strong netting which the radar technicians say would be okay. The radar boys wish to say something. Thank you, sir."

"We looked at the wrecked Swordfish and we think we can salvage one good radar set plus spares. We have to place the radar set with its cyclotron next to the radar aerial radome; the nearer the better. The cyclotron is a particle accelerator that produces microwaves which is the secret that makes our radar work. But microwaves are so short that they cannot be conveyed by copper or aluminum wiring. They propagate through a square tube we call a waveguide. We can fit a suitable one close to the rotating aerial bowl in the radome.

"We also need a long lead down to the monitors or screens in the wheelhouse and the bridge. These leads also have to be special. They are known as coaxial cables. We have a spare coil which is enough for our purpose. If everything can be fixed properly, which our ship's rigger says he can do, then we can do our side of your plan, so all in all, we think we can do it! As the weather is still not too bad, the sooner we start the better."

I looked at each of them and they all gave their approval. I looked at our commander who said that he would tell the captain and he thanked all concerned.

We did not have long to wait. The captain requested that I come and see him on his bridge where Hans and the officer-of-the-watch were also present. He told me that he fully agreed with the technicians. We should start forthwith but that he wished me to take overall control, which I agreed to.

He went to the steps leading down to the wheelhouse and shouted something. The four technicians clattered up the steps to the bridge where he told them his final decision and wished us all good luck. We retired to the flight deck.

This whole process took on a life of its own. The electrical/radar boys started with work on the power supply, laying cables and related activities, while the ships rigger brought up his tools, three safety harness, and with the help of one of the other boys, prepared the top of the bridge for the anchoring the radar radome.

I went up with him to discuss the best position of the radome and left them to it. They were keen and interested in what they were going to do and learn from each other. For those times this was secret state-of-the-art of electronics. The magic word was radar.

They were hard working chaps. From time to time, I had to remind them to observe safety standards or help them over a particular technical detail. We had plenty of onlookers, who were intrigued by the idea that we were actually building a small radar station. With all this activity, I was excused from flying duties which I felt created some bad feelings. They thought I had found a good scheme to avoid them.

It was completed in three days' time. The speed was due to the fact that these Technicians had already put things together or prepared for it before the final go-ahead was given. I watched them carefully everyday and saw the final test coming and was there to try it. We had some minor setbacks and had to tune the equipment for maximum picture clarity. All of a sudden, there it was! The five of us gave a yell of delight seeing the convoy around our ship except for a sector behind the ship that was screened off by the signal light behind the radar radome.

We switched off to let the captain and our flight commander try it out and see for themselves. In the meantime, the weather had deteriorated. It was overcast and misty which diminished the view from our ship but not from our radar set!

Both the captain and our flight commander came up the steps to the bridge. We requested that the captain inaugurate his radar set. I showed him the main switch for the radar set. He switched in on, then switched the bridge monitor on. The delight on his face was worth a million when he saw the small light points on the screen indicating the total convoy. "There is your convoy, sir," I said. For those times, this was the wonder of the world!

"I am astonished; I'm gob smacked; you must teach me to read it!"

"Captain," I said, "the radar screen reads like a clock. Twelve o'clock is dead-ahead, that line of light turning clockwise is a replica of your microwave-beam transmitted by your aerial. You can faintly hear your aerial rotating on top of this bridge. When this beam hits something like a ship, its echo bounces back to your radar set aerial and is shown on your screen. All this happens at the speed of light. Every time the beam hits a target, that light beam on your screen will light up its position and. before that point of light dies down, it will hit it again and again and again and makes it look like a spot of light.

"This screen is made for aircraft, so it is small. But look carefully. The rim is engraved with degree markings, so you can take a bearing on it. Finally, you can control your light brightness and contrast with those two small little knobs at the bottom of your monitor. The monitor in the wheelhouse is the same as on the bridge. It is switched on and off with the other toggle switch. Both are clearly marked. We have sufficient spares to keep it running.

"If not in use, may I suggest it is switched off? I wish you Godspeed with this radar set. Thank you, sir," I said and stepped back.

While the job itself was a small but interesting one, the five of us who had planned it and made it work were as proud as peacocks!

The weather and the ocean had deteriorated to the point of a howling gale with high waves, low clouds, bad visibility and lashing rains. From time to time there was a lull with a watery sun coming through as we approached Nova Scotia. We passed Sable Island in the distance. It was out of sight of the convoy but in easy flying distance.

We entered the German U-boat hunting grounds where the Germans had made many a successful kill of unsuspecting seamen of the merchant shipping along the American and Canadian coast. The Germans relied on espionage through careless talk by coastal shippers or took it for granted that all convoys from Europe to America had to leave and arrive from or to certain ports. Thus Halifax, New York and other similar ports were certainties to find shipping coming or going.

Our two MAC ships were placed on high alert with near constant patrolling, night or day; good weather or bad. It was now mid-November with snow and ice bothering our flight deck crew who had to get us airborne and patch up their aircraft, with chewing gum if need be.

Don't forget the Batsman and his mates who had to stand on deck in ice cold weather to get us safely on board or wait for us in the catwalk, the narrow steel cage around the flight deck, where you could stand safely or duck if the bits and tatters started flying through the air when aircraft made a bad landing.

We wrecked the remaining two aircraft in this atrocious weather. With the MAC Macoma wallowing in high seas, our pilots and Batsmen did their utmost to get planes on board. They left three hours earlier in bad but reasonable conditions.

They both landed badly and were thrown into the crash barrier shearing off their starboard wings. Luckily there were no fatalities, only minor cuts and bruises

We were in Canadian waters and were met by two Canadian destroyers. They were hardly visible in this murky weather with light snow coming down. Our captain was delighted with his radar set which still worked perfectly. I had the notion that he would like to keep it if the Netherlands Navy allowed it: I wished him well!

Escort carrier in convoy in rough weather and high seas in the North Atlantic Ocean. Coming back from patrol, the carrier would normally not be in the same position as where the plane had taken off, as the convoy would have progressed on a course that could have been changed without the aircrew being informed. Because of Radio-silence-in war-time, the weather could have changed for the worse and E.T.A. (estimated time of arrival), the convoy could possibly not be seen. A square search had to be made to hopefully find the convoy and its carrier. If the weather was bad the pilot would have to land on a deck that was moving wildly. It was thanks to the proficiency of the Fleet Air Arm pilots and the Flight Deck Crew that such landings were possible. There were times that the aircraft crash landed.

Sequel

We arrived at Halifax, Nova Scotia, Canada, on November 30, 1944, in the early morning and just managed to enjoy seeing a coast full of light from lampposts along invisible streets in the far distance, from buildings and factories and eventually from harbor installations. Since 1939 and 1940, we had not seen any village or city lights or lights from houses or lights of any sort, from the air or on the ground. To arrive at a continent where blackout was unknown was like a child's feeling of going to a circus. A sort of wonderment was that this still existed! We quickly got used to it. When we arrived at the quayside in Plymouth harbor, and moored fore and aft, I saw our wrecked Swordfish Mark III being craned ashore onto large flatbed lorries for replacement.

Our flight commander called us to the wardroom and told us that he received a message from the Royal Canadian Navy inviting our flying crew to join them for a few days to give us a break after our harrowing passage. He would like to keep one crew on board and allow the other three pilots and three navigators to accept the Canadian invitation.

"Any volunteers to stay?"

"No."

"Oh well, where are the dice? We'll throw for it!" he said.

The outcome was that Eddie and Taco stayed to attend to flight and flying matters, such as receiving four other aircraft, spares, flight deck repairs.

Hans told us to dress in our best uniforms and prepare an overnight bag with underwear and toilet articles for a week at the most. We had to escort the next convoy back to England if the replacement aircraft were on board, checked, tuned and prepared for flight.

The next morning Canadian sailors came on board to collect our night bags. To our surprise, their NCO had a big box of Royal Canadian Naval officer's fur caps with fur flaps that covered the ears. To our further surprise, he had the Royal Netherlands Naval cap badge already sewn on it they looked very smart! We were requested to leave our normal peak caps behind and to wear those forceps instead. Further inland the temperatures could go as low as ten degrees Celsius (twenty-five degrees Fahrenheit) during the day and twenty degrees Celsius (three degrees Fahrenheit) at night. This will freeze your earlobes as stiff as glass and when broken, they bleed all over when you enter a warm place.

He showed us how to wear them officially with the earflaps up and with the earflaps down covering the ears and clipped under the chin. Our flight commander was coming with us which made a group of seven Dutch officers as guest of the RCN.

The NCO told us that two official cars were waiting for us at the quayside. We put on our greatcoats, gloves and our new forceps and trooped down the gangway to the waiting cars.

Two smartly uniformed drivers saluted us, and we were on our way to the RCNAS (Royal Canadian Naval Air Station) where we boarded a Douglas troop carrier converted into a pleasant passenger plane. We were welcomed by a lieutenant commander pilot and six lieutenant pilots of the Canadian Navy. They informed us that we were on a flight to Montreal. Once airborne, the plane's two pilots took turns coming to the cabin to say "Hello," and wish us a pleasant stay.

It was a most pleasant and friendly flight with coffee and cakes and a chit-chat. They were eager to hear about the other side of the ocean. When they heard that two of us had escaped from German-occupied Netherlands, they were intrigued and wanted to know more. Jack and I were the only two officers who were wearing a medal ribbon. Our flight commander pointed out to them that this had to stop. German espionage, if they discovered where we were and what we were doing, could place our families in grave danger. The names we gave to the Canadian Press were bogus ones.

Montreal is a large city in a French speaking Canadian Province. When we arrived at the RCNAS HMS Donnacona, Montreal, we noticed that everything was bilingual; French and

English. But the population spoke French, felt French and acted as if they were French and proud of it!

We ended up at a most impressive luxury hotel. In a massive reception area, we were welcomed by two captains of the RCN who were our hosts. They wished us a pleasant and relaxing stay after the harrowing Atlantic crossing and escorting a convoy without losing one merchant ship.

The details of the next five days could fill pages that are outside the scope of this missive. I have curtailed this to short remarks as follows:

Arrival day. We settled in and decided to see the city. We found outside very cold and requested the doorman to call us a taxi:

"Taxi; oh no sir, there are two naval cars in our car parking area awaiting your pleasure. Please take the lift down to the third level and I'll tell them you're coming." And so it went with everything; we seemed to have landed on cloud nine.

Second day. We went to the Royal Netherlands Embassy to have lunch with the Netherlands Consul. He stood in for our ambassador who was on an official visit in the USA. Again, we met the press who took pictures and then discretely left.

Third day. The Canadian Naval pilots took us to an International Ice Hockey match in a huge sport stadium. It was between the Canadian and American Navies. We have never seen such a rough game, but we enjoyed every minute of it.

Fourth and Fifth days. All seven of us were invited to stay with seven important personalities, one of us to one person.

We waited for them in our room until the telephone called us down to the reception area to meet them. I was introduced to the chief justice, an older man with graying hair, tall with an aristocratic bearing and mannerisms who turned out to be a lovely man. He took me to his mansion outside the city in the forest. The snow was packed high, but the roads were scraped clean of loose snow while the cars had chains fitted round their tires. He drove carefully and as we arrived, a servant took over the keys of his car. We entered his house his wife was awaiting us.

She was a charming person who introduced me to her daughter who was, I guessed, of my age. He spoke to me as if he was my uncle and said, "May we call you by your first name?"

I told him that my nick-name in my squadron was Tip as Christiaan sounded too formal which made them smile.

"Nickname, what a suitable expression. We would call it a sobriquet; one is never too old to learn. We speak French at home, but we all speak good English including Mr. Thomas. My manservant is called Mr. Thomas. He will make your bed and clean your room. May I ask you to take of your uniform jacket. It's not only too formal but also too warm for our house. Also, your tie and move around with an open neck shirt. Have you got another pair of trousers? If not, we are about the same size. I'll tell Mr. Thomas to see if he can help you. Your uniform will be in good hands with him. You have noticed that our houses are very warm, even the less well-off have underground steam pipes feeding their central heating system in the center of our city. So, we move around our houses in very near summer clothes and have fur over clothes when we move outside.

"In your room you will find a pair of fur trousers, fur boots, a fur overcoat, a fur ice cap and a pair of snow goggles. Try them on and see if they fit. Otherwise Mr. Thomas will have them changed. We will go hunting tomorrow but will not take you too far as walking in the snow can be very tiring. We hope you to have a restful stay with us."

And so it went on; I was being spoiled until we all went to my hotel on the sixth morning to have our breakfast and gather to be taken to the airport. It became a jolly affair at the hotel with all Dutch flyers meeting again with our hosts and their families. Everyone decided to see us off at the airport so off we went in convoy to the airport where we said "Goodbye" and "Adieu." At the last moment we were given parcels and carry bags with all sorts of goodies, chocolate bars, bananas, oranges and items that we had been deprived of for many years and could only dream of.

What a farewell that was! How generously we had been pampered and feasted!

Sequent

As soon as we arrived at Halifax RCNA that the MAC Macoma had received four new replacement Swordfish Mark III with all the spares, the flight deck was repaired, and the tanker was topped up with ship engine diesel oil and aircraft engine fuel. We were ordered to join and escort a large convoy of sixty ships with many American Liberty ships carrying Army Nurses, troops, tanks, canon, jeeps, ammunition, food, and industrial material. This convoy was already on its way east and the MAC Macoma hastily drew anchor to join them. They had also received eight other Royal Netherlands Naval Fliers from MAC Gadila to replace us and had taken off Eddie and Taco.

Our new carrier was the MAC Gadila, lying at anchor in the bay. We found Eddie and Taco who had done some sterling work on the MAC Macoma acting as overseers, pointing out what had to be done, checking incoming spares. We were now together with our complete team of fliers and with four good Swordfish Mark III.

We had come back just in time as we felt the anchor chain rattling and off we went to join another massive convoy with many American Liberty ships.

The date was December 25, 1944, and we were back in the groove. By now that came naturally to us. We had to get down to brass tacks and the reality that we were still at war with a very clever enemy who would stop at nothing, so we had to get started and try to prevent the German U-boats from damaging our convoys.

The end of the Battle of the Atlantic drew to a close and the war ended on VE Day, August 5, 1945, the U boats were instructed by German Admiral Karel Donitz to surrender to any Allied warship by flying a black flag.

In the final tally, the U-boats sank two thousand six hundred and three merchant ships and one hundred and seventy-five Allied warships. They lost seven hundred and eighty-four U-boats out of one thousand one hundred and sixty-two built. Out of the forty thousand nine hundred men of the German U-boat Service nearly twenty-six thousand died and over five thousand were taken prisoner. On the Allied side, the price we paid was roughly thirty thousand killed.

Before I become tedious and move too far with the dreary convoy story, let me reflect upon flying patrols over an endless ocean, over enormous tidal waves with their deep troughs, towering crests, changing and treacherous weather conditions which, at times, look so mild and friendly with wonderful blue skies but with different wind velocities at different heights of flight and with none of our present-day gadgets. That was a fight for your life against cold and tiredness, against the concern that the weather would cut you off from your convoy and aircraft carrier, your only home in this universe! And yet, you are advised that, "There is nothing to fear but fear itself," until it hits you!

The sight of your convoy when flying low under low cloud cover, on your return flight after a three or three-and-a-half-hour stint, through bad visibility, is a feeling of such relief that beggars description.

Then your pilot still has to get your plane safely onto the flight deck. Well, that's his department! With utter faith in your pilot's ability you await your destiny with equanimity!

We reached Ireland and flew to our home base RNAS Maydown. On arrival, were told that we had two weeks leave and could make use of two older Swordfish Mark I to fly to London to "let our hair down."

Back in London, we housed again at Regents Park Hotel near Piccadilly Circus, which suited us fine!

I had lived in a news vacuum for so long that I was oblivious of worldly affairs. I knew little, of the war except for major Allied gains and Russian advances in the East. We were kept and trained by the Navy and did not have a care in the world for our next meal, clothing, and would be useless if we had to do such mundane things. Even my hotel was paid for by a magical uncle. What did concern me was what was happening in The Netherlands. My parents did not know where I was, what I did or if I was still alive. I was equally in the dark.

We never received mail. We envied our British counterparts when post was handed out and they retired to enjoy the written reunion with their loved ones. But we, of course, showed our stiff upper lip!"

On my first night of my leave, I went to The Netherlands Club. Coming into the bar I saw to my great surprise Ome Jan sitting on a barstool in the uniform of a naval commander.

As a reminder, *Ome Jan, or Uncle John,* was the nickname we gave our Director of the Navigational College in Den Helder before the war.

It was mid-winter and I still had on my warm greatcoat. I went up to him and asked him if he was Commander Middendorp, or as known to us in Den Helder, Ome Jan. That surprised him. It slowly dawned on him that I must have been one of his students. He told me to take off my greatcoat and join him for a drink. I did, showing him my full uniform. That was his next surprise. He looked me over and said, "Wow. Lieutenant Observer of the Fleet Air Arm with the Bronze Cross. Where did you buy all that? Come closer and let me introduce you!"

After a couple of drinks, he invited me to have dinner with him. Going upstairs to the dining room we met some friends of his who were in mufti. They insisted that we have dinner with them.

Mr. and Mrs. van Jaarsveld were delightful company. I soon learned that he was a Director of Unilever and she was a University Lecturer in Greek and Latin. Yet they were so natural and friendly. However, they were far more interested in my job in the Fleet Air Arm. When they learned that I was on leave after a spell in the North Atlantic convoy escort system, they invited me to stay with them until my leave expired rather than stay in that dreadful (their words) hotel.

I said a fond farewell to Ome Jan Middendorp. Taking me aside, he said, "Take it easy and take great care, the war is nearly over. Don't worry about telling Headquarters. I'll tell them where you are. I wish you Godspeed!" I never saw him again.

Mr. van Jaarsveld had an official car parked outside. It stood there lonely in the street as very few people had such a privilege in war time. After checking out of the Regents Park Hotel, we drove to the North of London to their villa. It was beautifully furnished in Dutch style and surrounded by a large well-kept garden. My bedroom with bathroom attached was spacious and comfortable. I thought that I was dreaming with such luxury around me after years of the harsh conditions I was used to.

The van Jaarsvelds were tall as most Hollanders are and liked to jog around their leafy neighborhood to keep fit. They enquired where my family was and were surprised to hear that I was an Engelandvaarder having escaped from German-occupied Holland.

I told them that I did not have a clue how my family was or even if they were still alive. They caught me up-to-date with world affairs in general, the war in Europe and the situation in The Netherlands in particular.

They were preparing for their return as soon as possible. Did I have any plans? I told them, when my leave period was over I would fly back to Northern Ireland to pick up the latest Swordfish Mark III and to join a MAC ship to escort another big convoy back to Canada and afterwards to escort another big convoy back to Scotland. That would see me back roughly in April or May 1945.

We were prepared and trained to chase German U-boats when Germany capitulated and prevent them from escaping to South America. All this would take some time and I had no idea when I would see my family again. They promised that they would see my parents and tell them all about me which was comforting!

We parted on a similar note. They took me to my airport, Great West Aerodrome, which became London Heathrow Airport. They stayed and waved until we took off. Great West Aerodrome belonged to the Fairey Company Limited where they built and tested the Swordfish aircraft. If there is a great Valhalla of the skies, next to the hall of fame of slain warriors, there should be one for aircraft. Sharing honors with the greatest is the Fairey Swordfish, which had a legendary history. Its achievements were second to none and it was affection ally known by all that flew her as the String Bag.

World War II did not peter out or come to a slow conclusion like World War I when the defeated German Armed Forces never surrendered but walked out of Belgium and France and back to Germany.

Based on their massive losses in Russia and at sea, in late 1944 and early 1945 it looked as if the final conclusion was near. But the German motto and rule of conduct was; we will never capitulate. They did not capitulate. With a "God is with us" on their belt buckles, they fought until the bitter end on land and at sea! They were totally defeated in the air.

Prang

My dependable pilot Rego had made arrangements with RNAS HMS Nightjar near Inskip, to top up our aviation fuel tank and have a bite to eat. When we arrived at approximately 11:00 hours, circling their control tower, we received a jolly welcome as old friends. The fuel tender was waiting for us with some aircraft mechanics standing ready to give the engine a quick check and to do whatever Rego wanted seen to.

In my ponderous flying outfit, I wobbled my way clumsily to the control tower to get the latest weather report and other useful information. On my return, Rego was waiting for me with some NAAFI girls in their van, hot tea and sandwiches. They went down as a real treat.

After getting the green light from the control tower, we took off and flew past the Isle of Man over the Irish Sea into the Northern Channel, then turned west to Rathin Island, then south over Lough Foyle to land at our home base RNAS Maydown at about 15:00 hours.

We received orders to be ready, to join MAC Macoma in the Firth of Clyde by 06:00 hours the next morning. We were destined to escort a large convoy of some sixty merchantmen and eight escorts to Halifax, Canada.

Most of the merchant ships were sailing in ballast and riding high as Britain had very little to export other than disabled and wounded American and Canadian servicemen. On the return journey bound for the Clyde, the ships were heavily laden and lumbering with food, war material and troops.

The date was April 3, 1945. Our convoy arrived in Canadian waters twenty-two days later. It was a routine journey with lots of patrols, nothing exciting and good weather. We arrived at Halifax where a large convoy was gathering, mainly Liberty ships carrying American troops, equipment and supplies for the Second Front. The MAC Macoma was given just enough time to get supplies, diesel oil, aircraft fuel, and spare parts for our Swordfish. A team of

Canadian naval aircraft technicians came aboard to inspect our four Swordfish/ We were off again to escort this large convoy. It had three MAC ships operating as a unit with twelve Swordfish.

We were very excited with the news of VE-day, April 8, 1945. It seemed so far away; as if it had happened on another planet. As I looked out over miles and miles of an unending lonely stretch of ocean from horizon to horizon, it seemed that time had created a barrier between past and present. My parents, family and friends were in a dream world. We were totally unaware of what had happened in Holland in that terrible winter of hunger and sadness. In those last months of German occupation, the Allied Operation Manna had thrown out food parcels from low flying bombers.

The German U-boat menace had abated considerably. Most people had the notion that the Battle of the Atlantic was over in 1943. In fact, after VE-day, one hundred and fifty-six U-boats surrendered in their own good time as they saw fit. Some even had a last fling by sinking a merchant ship out of pure spite and malice. Some tried to escape to South America, with as many persons as their U-boat could safely hold and would put up a fight if they were not fast enough to dive out of harm's way.

The Allied navies were taking no chances, but it was soon over, and our convoy seemed to be the last one. However, discipline was discipline and we went through all the motions of the war time drill with daily patrols.

The weather turned bad with storm, rain and tremendous waves which tended to create more stragglers than usual. What we hated most was to look for them to the rear of the convoy. We were lucky that the storm wind came from the west towards our convoy which was east bound.

Returning from one such stragglers search, flying under low cloud, heavy rain and a strong west wind, we looked with trepidation at the mountainous waves which had developed since we had left MAC Macoma. We did not see our convoy until we were nearly on top of her. And which was our carrier? Or was it one of the other carriers?

The Macoma was turning into the west wind to receive us when we noticed a corvette near her. We realized that by sailing West the Macoma would leave the eastbound convoy on her own. That would require the protection of an Escort. It was up to my pilot to get us down safely on a flight deck tossed about by heavy seas.

We got the green light from the bridge and Rego made his landing approach watching the Batsman like a hawk. His job was very difficult under the circumstances. He could feel the ships movements but had to keep a keen eye on the incoming Swordfish and be guided by another batsman who could watch the waves and the bow for him. All went well until the last moment when the arrester hook was just about to catch the ship's arrester wires. Right then the ship's stern fell away and we stalled and sailed straight into the crash barrier. Our right wings were sheared off by the island and all sorts of pieces of aircraft were flying around what a hell of a prang!

I was blissfully unaware of all the commotion. The asbestos man (in a fireproof suit) from the rescue party had dragged me out of what was left of the plane into the hands of the rescue party. I woke up below the flight deck in a makeshift sickbay behind a curtain in a passage with a bad pain in my back. I saw Rego looking at quite concerned asking me how I felt. I told him about my painful back. He called the orderly, who was also a paramedic. (We had no doctor on board.) He took off my blanket to have a look. That was when I noticed that I did not have a stitch on. I was told they were in tatters, but not to worry, I would not need them for a while! The orderly gave me something to drink that put me fast asleep, which was a blessing.

On waking up and calling out for a bottle to relieve myself, the orderly told me that I was cut and bruised badly on my face and lower back and had possibly damaged my spine in the lumbar region. But, without x-rays that was just a guess. With permission of the captain or our flight commander he would put me in a plaster cast. Both officers came down to see me. The captain had contacted the doctor on the leading Destroyer of the Commodore. He told him the plaster cast had to be put on with me in a stretched position. In the absence of a hospital bed with a stretching facility, I should be hung by my wrist so that my body weight would stretch me and keep me stretched until the cast set.

A steel hook was welded on the steel ceiling near my bed and a small block and tackle rigged. They put a towel round my wrists before fixing a rope round it. It was hooked up with the block and tackle and with assistance I went up until my toes just touched the deck. I was given a strong painkiller, but it was still very uncomfortable as the orderly put on wet cast bandages round my body from my armpits to my hips. Two air blowers were used to blow air onto the cast from the front and the back to speed up the drying process. There I was; a plaster of Paris dummy, as heavy as a block cement. They tenderly put me back to bed on my back.

It certainly helped. I had little or no pain except if I laughed with my flying colleagues. They all come to sign my white cast and write something funny or naughty. Commander Flying came to see me and told everybody to leave me as I needed to rest. Before he left, he told me that we were nearing home waters and they would fly me to the RAF Coastal Command Station at Oban in Scotland where they had a hospital. They would give me a good examination to find out what was wrong with me. He told me not to worry, just have a good rest and he would organize everything.

When I woke up, I wondered where I was. Then I felt my plaster cast and most of my face with swollen lips and painful mouth. I called the orderly with a blubbery mouth and a sailor put his head through the curtain and told me he would call him. He came in through the curtain in his pajamas and told me that it was still night and asked if he could be of help? I asked him what had happened to my face and mouth and he replied that he was very sorry that it was a mess. It would require a dentist to look at it. We were approaching Ireland and they would fly me to a hospital in Scotland. Was I in pain? Please take it easy and relax. He got me some sleeping tablets.

When I woke up again, there was Rego's smiling face. He told me that he would fly me to Oban and that everything was organized. They would hoist me into my cockpit as I could still sit up and that all my belongings would be stowed in the gunner's cockpit.

"Don't you worry old mate, you're out of the war now. Don't try to talk. I'll do all the talking. You're not fit to make a speech with your swollen lips and two blue eyes you're a real beauty. What can I get you?"

The orderly came in and said, "Sorry sir, no liquor for this gentleman. He's on baby food and may I respectfully ask you to leave? He needs all the rest he can get!"

"Wow," said Rego, "you are being mollycoddled. See you."

I came up the next morning, carried onto the flight deck on a stretcher. I was well sedated; all wrapped up in a blanket, with a leather flying helmet and goggles on. I noticed that there was only one Swordfish ready to fly. I was told by the crew who were handling me that all the flyers including Rego had left for our home base at RNAS Maydown. My pilot would be the Commander Flying Hans van Vlaander.

I was hoisted up by a crane in a sitting position and slowly lowered into my cockpit assisted by two aircraft mechanics. They strapped me in, and for good measure, padded me with bed pillows, connected my helmet leads to the intercom socket, and wished me all the best and a speedy recovery. I soon fell asleep until the intercom with Hans's voice asked if I was okay and comfortable. On my grunt, which he took as an affirmative, the engine started and the Swordfish vibrated in the good old way that was assuring to my sleepy mind. I fell asleep again not even noticing our take off.

I woke up when hands took off my straps and prepared me for another hoist to take me out of my cockpit. Off I went up and down to another stretcher and into an ambulance. It ended when I was put into a hospital bed where I was washed and tucked in. I was hardly aware of any of this. When I woke up, I realized what had happened and where I was; on my back, in a plaster cast with a nurse trying to read all the nonsense my colleagues had written on it!

After X-rays were taken, followed by a thorough check up by a doctor and a dentist, I was told that my lower spine in the lumbar region was damaged but not broken. An operation on the spine was out of the question as it could paralyze me. I would have to wear a special surgical corset with all my movements out of bed, but that would not cripple me. Rather it would assist me to prevent pain in my movements. That corset would be discreet, not noticeable when wearing a jacket. It was already on order from a specialist firm in London. I was grounded and could not continue my flying career in the forces but could possibly be of use in some other discipline. Otherwise my cuts and bruises would heal in time.

The dentist told me that I must have been hit on the side of my face as the skin inside the mouth was badly cut but would heal in time. Some back teeth had to be pulled as they had been nearly shattered. There were no bones broken but some teeth needed to be rebuilt to save them. You were lucky! We started on this work the next day. I have never been scared of dying but dreaded the aftereffects of a bad accident. As the dentist said, I could count myself very lucky!

Commander Flying, Hans van Vlaander, came to see me two weeks later. I was doing my walking exercises. He told me that London had read my medical report and wondered if I would consider to be trained as an air signal officer as they badly needed someone with flying experience. But the war is over, I replied.

He said, "Yes, here in Europe. But we still have to fight the Japs and we are getting a proper Escort Carrier."

What a thought! More war and I was still a conscript and under military law. The prestigious rank of signal officer in the Navy was not something to sneeze at so I agreed to be trained as an air signal officer. I would be promoted to the rank of senior lieutenant! This five months course would be at the Naval Air Signal School at HMS Condor RNAS Arbroath.

Ltz. Waarnemer 2e.klasse OC (Senior Lieutenant Observer / Navigator)
C.Gutteling BK

Verbindings-Officier (Signals Officer)
on the Escort Carrier Hr.Ms."Karel Doorman"
(ex HMS."Nairana" - white-eagle in Maori)

April 1947

Postscript

My Brevet or Authoritative Certificate conferring my standing as air signal officer was awarded to me on November 3, 1945. I soon got my second stripe as senior lieutenant. It was more of a technical study than a physical training course. It dealt with the basic electronic technicalities of the latest state-of-the-art radio, radar and ASDIC equipment and their efficacy and limitations. Signal codes and code books which included flag signals was all very interesting, but at times, a real slog up the learning curve. Especially when I had to battle with the English sea language and technical jargon.

I was told that I was due for a month's leave in The Netherlands to see my family. For that privilege I had to get myself on a plane from the North Aerodrome, northeast of London to fly to the Royal Netherlands Naval Air Station at Valkenburg near The Hague. This was a sentimental journey! All the necessary instructions and warrants would reach me within a short time. I was overjoyed. Home at last, if there was a home left. Who would be still alive after that terrible Hunger Winter of 1944? Over two hundred thousand people were saved from starvation by the British and American bombers in Operation Mana. They flew at two hundred feet or less, at one hundred fifty miles per hour dropping three hundred and fifty thousand food parcels instead of bombs. This lasted over for one week over an area from Den Helder in the north to the province of Zeeland in the south.

Few people would talk about it or had the knowledge to talk about it. They just shrugged their shoulders. I was one of them wondering what I would find.

It started on September 17, 1944, with the Allied Arnhem fiasco (*A Bridge too far*) where the Germans counter-attacked in strength and made the Allies withdraw. They left a chaotic mess which the Germans could hardly handle. They only looked after their own interests as they were cut off from the German Reich who was in deep trouble with the Russian onslaught. The German occupation of Holland had the lowest priority. The Germans were soon out of food and tampered with the Dutch food supply. German soldiers confiscated or stole food from the Dutch. Their daily food ration was soon reduced to thirteen hundred calories. To make things worse, the German troops started flooding the country by opening the dikes and cutting communications. They feared a Dutch uprising or Allied attack. Thousands of people were marooned.

There was also a scarcity of coal and wood to keep the houses warm and deforestation of Holland started. Electricity was cut off, candles were not available, and people stayed in their beds to get some comfort in a very cold winter. Shoe leather was not available as the Germans needed that for their troops. People started mending shoes with leather from handbags until many had to go barefoot.

People ate bulbs and became so emaciated and weak that they were unable to bury their dead. Streets had dying people unable to go any further; there were dead people in the canals who slowly drifted out to sea.

Only those who saved food and fought to preserve what they had in hiding places survived. It was a total destruction of society. It became every man or family for themselves.

The unending tragedy became known to the Allied generals and President Roosevelt But they were not interested in or incapable of assisting until the German Reichskommissar Dr. Artur von Seyss-Inquart contacted the Netherlands government in London to set up a scheme to prevent a total catastrophe. This became known as Operation Manna. The German Army Command in The Netherlands ordered their anti-aircraft guns not to fire on the low flying Allied bombers. The aircrew flying the British and American bombers were volunteers and were very moved by what they saw as they flew low dropping three hundred and fifty thousand food parcels. They launched the first flight on April 29, 1945.

The Navy did me proud with a first-class train ticket to London and chauffeured cars to and from the railway stations. I arrived at North Aerodrome where I had a late breakfast waiting for the call to board my aircraft which would fly me home.

Arriving at Valkenburg Airport, I found it modern and well equipped as The German Luftwaffe had enlarged and modernized it. An immaculately uniformed sailor helped me with my luggage to his well cleaned and glossy looking car and off we went into The Hague. When we arrived at my parent's house the sailor told me not to worry with my luggage as he would carry it to the front door and announce my arrival. But I told him that I would do the announcing.

I rang the doorbell and my mother opened the door. I so tongue-tied that I just took my cap off and she said, "Tip, it's you!" We embraced, and I was home!

This was the end of my war and my beginning again.

Epilogue

The Meaning of it All?

No one can predict how much difference one's actions will or can make to a war effort or if those actions were necessary or useful at all. The risks, the duty was for whom or for what? After all, we were small parts in a large whole. If you wish, small cogs in enormous clockwork.

What we did can only be viewed in the context of the world events in our time. Since then a barrier has been created between past and present; between my generation and the contemporary; between raw crunching reality and the academic suppositional.

For instance, we were young and easily intimidated, influenced or coerced; whatever case may have applied. Or diametrically the opposite, we become furiously obsessed with hatred of the enemy who had caused the destruction or retardation of our studies or our jobs and thereby our future and had destroyed our homes and livelihood; or had killed one or more of our family members or friends.

Whatever the causes, The Netherland's population was bisected in pro and anti-German feelings. The pros favoring and siding openly with the Germans. The antis carefully and quietly licking their wounds and secretly planning against the German war effort. If possible, without being shot or imprisoned. Others lived quietly without upsetting anyone by word of mouth or deed and praying the Lord for deliverance.

Every belligerent country that took taken part in World War II has its own version of the war. They give prominence to the parts they played. At times, this borders on a fixation. For instance, the words concentration camps refers only to those organized by the enemy. In principle, there is little to remonstrate on things said as long as one can distinguish impartial facts from patriotic comment, such as: "My country right or wrong," or the posture of denial or political manipulation. The art is to be able to distinguish reality from rhetoric. That means knowledge and understanding of the opposite view. Mockery ends where understanding begins.

As time passes, uncritical attitudes appear to multiply as later generations lose sight of wartime attitudes of mind and complexities. For instance, Western apologists rarely explore the Soviet role. It was enormous. The Western role was respectable but modest in the European land theatre. Many thinking people are still trying to make any sense out of it all and many are still biased by their upbringing and nationality.

ANNEX

The Wrens

By September 1944, the strength of the Women's Royal Naval Services or Wrens had built up from nil in June 1939 to its wartime peak of about seventy-five thousand officers and ratings filling ninety different categories of duty and fifty different branches.

There were some reactionary males who looked on the Wrens as a monstrous regiment of women, like the grizzled old chief cook who said, "Of all the 'orrible things this 'orrible war has done, these 'orrible women are the 'orriblest."

In reality, tribute must be paid to the Wrens for their superlative contribution to the war effort!

Anybody with any sense at all could see as the war progressed, that there were large areas of life and duties in the Navy and in the Fleet Air Arm which simply would not function without the contribution of the Wrens!

By the end of the war, there were few aspects of the Service which the Wrens had not stamped with their own individual flavor.

The first categories of Wrens in October 1939 included secretaries, cypherers, coders, clerks, accountants, typists, telephone operators, signaler's, motor transport drivers, and cooks. By 1940 Wrens serving in virtually every naval establishment and base in the United Kingdom, from Cornwall up to the Orkneys and from Kent across to Northern Ireland. In 1941, the Wrens went abroad. The first draft of twelve cypher officers and ten Chief Wren's special operators were killed when the SS Aguila was torpedoed and sunk en route to Gibraltar. This was a shock the Navy felt like the loss of a major war vessel.

"It would be impossible to picture a finer company. We sent our best," wrote the Director Wrens at the time.

However, the undeterred Wrens were soon serving all over the world; in Egypt, North Africa, Washington, the Persian Gulf, Ceylon, India and Australia.

In 1942, the categories of Wren duties broadened to include radar operators, cinema operators, gunnery dome operators, recruiters, censors, submarine attack teacher operators, meteorological data plotters, operations room assistants, bomb range markers, vision testers, AA target operators, tailoresses, routing officers, intelligence officers, orthoptists, and boats' crews. Wrens worked the decoding machine for ULTRA.

For the Fleet Air Arm, Wrens packed parachutes and looked after safety equipment, maintained radios, engines, air frames and torpedoes, interpreted photo reconnaissance, instructed in escape and evasion techniques, and assisted in the teaching of Fighter Direction Officers.

They brought a touch of color and an element of intuitive feminine logic into an otherwise austere wartime scene. Generally, they had a higher boredom threshold than men, were meticulous about detail and liked to work a project through to its end.

Many a romance between Wrens and aircrew flourished on the bleak windswept tundras of Scottish airfields, in draughty hangars on the Welsh coast, on steamy verandahs in Delhi, in the tropically scented nights of Kandy, in the breezy heights of the control tower at Yeovilton. Squadrons gladly put on their number one uniforms and best drinking boots to celebrate marriages between aircrew and Wrens in all manner of places from Bournemouth to Boston, Bermuda to Bondi, and Bombay to Brawdy.

Some of the letters and poems which Wrens wrote have such keen perceptions they still touch the heart. One Third Officer WRNS (Woman's Royal Naval Services), but everyone said Wrens, American equivalent to Waves, serving at an air station in Ceylon, endured watching the pilot she hoped to marry die in a flying accident.

A poem she wrote in a Fleet Poetry Broadsheet published in Colombo in 1945 contains a truthful observation about the Fleet Air Arm, wrapped in authentic period language.

Fleet Flyer

> "Good show!" he said, leaned back his head and
>   laughed. "They're wizard types!" he said, and held
>   his beer.
> Steadily, he looked at it and gulped it down. Out of its
>   jam-jar he took a cigarette and blew a neat smoking
>   ring into the air.
> "After this morning's prang I've got the twitch; I
>   thought I'd had it in that teased out kite."
> His eyes were blue and older than his face. His single
>   stripe had known a lonely war, but all his talk and
>   movements showed his age.
> His whole life was the air and his machine. He had no
>   thought but of the latest "mod." His jargon was of
>   aircraft or of beer.
> "And what will you do afterwards?" I said, then saw
>   his puzzled face and caught my breath.
> There was no afterwards for him, but death.

There was also an ode to the thousands of women working in the Arms Industry, dated 1942, as follows:

> "It was the girl that makes the thing,
> that holds the oil, that oils the ring,
> that works the thingamabob,
> that's going to win the war."

In peace time all sailors, including WRNS and WRENS, from all over the world wore a black hat band that stated the name of the ship that they were stationed on. During, the war the name of the ship was replaced with a general title. For example, in Britain, HMS, which stands for Her Majesty Service was replaced with a hat band. If they were captured the identity of the ship or air station was not revealed. All names disappeared off rail stations, harbors and airports, and all names were replaced so the low flying planes would look for a name but all they could see was a number. This was done all over the world. Signs in large print, were placed on walls all over the world, stating "Careless Talk Cost Lives."

Battle of the Atlantic

How it started:

Shipping was Britain's lifeblood: all would be lost unless the convoy routes stayed open! It was Churchill's greatest worry and concern that Britain would be running out of food and have to sue for peace, which was tantamount to capitulation.

It was recognized that merchant shipping moved more safely in guarded convoys; a lesson Britain learned the hard way in World War I. But now, in World War II, when there were outdated arms, insufficient escorts and equipment to effectively guard all the convoys required to sustain the British Isles, the convoys faced new menaces including the Uboat Wolf Packs, magnetic mines, and air attack.

The Battle of the Atlantic started from the first day that Britain declared war, on September 3, 1939, at 11:15 a.m. The British liner Athenia, bound for Canada from Liverpool, was sunk by a German U-boat off the Scottish coast with the loss of one hundred and twelve lives out of one thousand four hundred passengers. This was followed on September 17, 1939, when the aircraft carrier HMS Courageous was sunk with the loss of five hundred and eighteen lives. Even more dramatic was the sinking of the battleship HMS Royal Oak in Scapa Flow, the Royal Navy's nearly impregnable anchorage in Orkney, Scotland, on October 14, 1939, taking with it eight hundred and thirty-three men.

One of the early convoys, SC7, was nearly home; its thirty-five merchant ships and three Escorts, consisting of two sloops and one corvette were about eight hundred kilometers northwest of Ireland but just outside the air cover range provided by the RAF Coastal Command. The German Navy had setup and organized their U-boat headquarters at Lorient, Brittany, in occupied France. Admiral Donitz had devised the new technique for U-boats known as the Wolf Pack, whereby U-boats could be quickly directed towards a target and carry out a mass attack.

One U-boat on the prowl, U48, in the dark before midnight had stumbled on convoy SC7 and had radioed its position, course, speed and size to Lorient. The U-boat Staff at Lorient headquarters directed seven more submarines to join U48. In the meantime, they had already sunk two merchant ships. The Wolf Pack was directed into the path of this convoy. The final result was plain carnage. This U-boat Wolf Pack sank a total of twenty merchant ships; only fifteen ships survived. SC7 was no longer a convoy, but a mass of sinking, burning and broken ships under a heavy pall of black smoke from burning wood and oil and men trying to survive in ice cold, oily burning water. None of the seven U-boats was lost.

As the seven U-boats slipped away from this carnage, Lorient radioed that another convoy was approaching, and the carnage began again.

German U-boat commanders called this period in October 1940 the happy time. During this time, they sunk 217 merchant ships.

The Allied navies had a bad year in 1941. The war of attrition which developed was to be decided as much by the competition in shipbuilding as by the exchanges of torpedoes and depth charges at sea. Grand Admiral Raeder of the German Navy calculated that, if Germany could sink an average of seven hundred thousand tons of Allied shipping per month for a year, Britain would be starved into submission.

Hitler, inflamed by Churchill's dogged refusal to capitulate, declared a total blockade of the British Isles on August 17, 1940. Things only got worse as German ship-building yards turned out more and more U-boats.

U-boats based in Brittany, occupied France, concentrated their attacks on the Gap in mid-Atlantic. The slow-moving convoys were not protected by air patrols operating from Canada and Greenland or by the RAF Coastal Command operating from Oban, Scotland.

Mass Wolf Pack night attacks caught the convoy escorts almost unprepared. ASDIC was useless against U-boats on the surface. There were no proper communications between escort vessels other than signal lamps using Morse code, sirens, flags and old-fashioned radiotelephones.

The scourge of the Atlantic was the Focke Wulf 200, the Condor. The German long range, three thousand five hundred and thirty kilometers, reconnaissance and bomber aircraft were fitted with forward firing twenty-millimeter cannons and a twin machinegun. They worked closely with Lorient and the U-boats and had a devastating effect on the convoys.

For a time, it looked as if the Germans might reach the desired sinking rate as the U-boats feasted hungrily in the Gap and on American shipping on the American eastern seaboard. By this time, Hitler had declared war with America.

The Battle of the Atlantic reached its climax when two hundred and forty U-boats operated in Wolf Packs from both sides of the Gap. Sailors called it Torpedo Junction.

Technology slowly did improve. Technology like ASDIC, Hedgehog mortars and surface radar and intensive retraining of Escort Commanders gained. What was most helpful was the breaking the German secret code used by the U-boats to communicate with Lorient. This was done at Bletchley Park in 1941. Another help was the capture of an Enigma coding machine and its handbook from a captured U-boat.

Increased numbers of Escorts began to have effect. Even so, one thousand six hundred and sixty-seven merchant ships were lost against eighty-seven U-boats. An interesting feature was the introduction of the CAM ship (Catapult Aircraft Merchantman). It met the threat of the Condor. These ships carried a Hawker Hurricane fighter aircraft which could be launched by catapult. This was expensive, as after the Hurricane fighter mission was complete it was ditched in the sea close to the CAM ship or any other escort vessel, so the pilot could be rescued. Alternatively, the pilot could parachute from it. In either case, the aircraft was lost.

The U-boat threat was also met by the introduction of Escort Carriers built in America from Liberty ships with a flight deck, hanger and all the extras required to run a carrier; such as extra tanks for aircraft fuel, ammunition and arms magazines, aircraft lift, and fire-fighting systems. However, there were not enough of them as Liberty ships were built mainly to augment the merchant fleet as fast as possible to keep up with the sinking rate. The Americans did this and more in three enormously large shipyards. They used standardized prefabricated sections for quick assembly at the yards.

In 1942, five hundred and ninety-seven, Liberty ships had been built. By July 1943, Allied ship building as a whole outstripped the number the U-boats sank. That saved the flow of supplies across the Atlantic.

Special mention should be made of the Short Sunderland which the Germans called the Flying Porcupine as it bristled with machineguns. In its final development it had eighteen machineguns. This plane was developed from a pre-war passenger flying boat and gave the RAF Coastal Command its first long distance capability of four thousand seven hundred kilometers. It first went into service in 1938 and the Mark V version was still in service in 1959. It carried a nine-hundred-kilogram bomb load. Almost seven hundred and fifty Sutherland's were built.

There were not enough of them to close the Gap. Land based aircraft could not reach this area where convoys and their escorts had to fend for themselves with dire consequences.

The turning point came in 1943. While March of that year was one of the blackest months, April brought considerable relief and in May the Germans lost more U-boats than Allied ships. This was the point when the Western Allies could begin to think confidently about transporting a major American army to Britain.

The sea war never stopped; it continued to 1945. But German attacks became less painful. Massive air patrols reduced the U-boat capabilities, while American shipyards were building three or four Liberty ships every day.

Overall, well over a hundred thousand Allied and German sailors perished.

The Karel Doorman (1889-1942) ship was named after Admiral, Karel Doorman. 1889-1942. In 1942 he became the commander of the Combined Striking Force which consisted of Australian, American, British, and Netherlands ships. On February 28,1942, he was killed in action on his cruiser Hr. Ms. De Rugter, the flag ship of this striking force. Two aircraft carriers were named after him.

I served on Hr. Ms. Karel Doorman from March 3, 1948. This was also the time that I was demobilized. The Karel Doorman was on loan from the British Navy to train Netherlands Navy personnel. It was previously the Escort-Carrier HMS Nairana. In the New Zealand Maori language, Nairana means white-tailed eagle. I went to Netherlands East India, now Indonesia. On my first visit to South Africa we entered the narrow basin of Simonstown on September 20, 1946. My second visit was on our return journey to South Africa when we entered the harbor of Cape Town on January 8, 1947. I served as a signal officer in charge of thirty-five men with the rank of senior lieutenant. My staff consisted of flag-signal/light-signal men who were stationed on the top bridge, radio telegraghist, electronic engineers, NCOs. It included air signals to keep in touch with her aircraft. This ship could have a total crew of one thousand men. We carried approximately nine hundred plus men, which included all personnel required to fly twenty Naval Spitfires with two cockpits; for pilot and navigator.

This ship was originally designed to be a fruit carrier with cooking facilities. But that changed with the escalating UBoat wars and the massive losses of Merchant Navy ships. She was completed to be a Convoy Escort-Carrier to work in the North Atlantic. She was originally to escort the Murmansk Convoys to North Russia. She was approximately one hundred and sixty meters long with a displacement of seventeen thousand ton. Her flight deck was nine meters above water level. The Karel Doorman was returned to the British Royal Navy in 1948 after I was demobilized in December 1947. She was rebuilt as a refrigerator ship again with accommodations for twelve passengers. She was completed in 1950 and rebaptised as Port Victor. She carried cooled and frozen meat. In 1962, she met a new Karel Doorman II in the Bay of Caraca on the island of Curacao in the Caribbean Sea.

The new Karel Doorman II was a proper light fleet carrier of the British Royal Navy known HMS Venerable of the Colossus Class. She was bought outright for about twenty-seven million pounds. She could carry up to forty aircrafts, normal loaded with thirty-six. She had a displacement of 13,190 tons; less than Karel Doorman I. She was originally designed to be a merchant ship with wide beam to carry cargo. She was officially taken over by the Royal Netherlands Navy in May 1948.

SWORDFISH
Major Achievements, Abridged

The Swordfish was just an aero-plane. Its legends and achievements were only as good as the skilled and gallant crews made them.

Sinking of the Bismarck

At 20:00 hours on May 26, 1941, in a combined attack on the world's most powerful battleship, the Bismarck, a Swordfish's torpedo wrecked Bismarck's steering. It was hopelessly and helplessly turning in circles awaiting its end. The final blows were given by the sixteen-inch guns from the British battleships HMS King George V, Prince of Wales and Rodney. It was 10:39 hours of May 27, 1941, when she went down with two thousand crew members. One hundred and ten survivors were picked up.

Night Attack on Taranto

On November 11, 1944, twenty-one Swordfish torpedo bearing bi-planes were available for the attack on Italy's naval harbor Taranto.

At 20:35 hours, the first wave of twelve Swordfish took off from HMS Illustrious stationed off the Greek island of Cephalonia 275 kilometers southeast of Taranto.

Just under two-and-a-half hours later they were approaching the Italian base when all hell broke loose with ack-ack fire. The Italians were alerted by their sound detectors, which ruined any chance of surprise. The attackers carried on undeterred. Two Swordfish dropped flares that bathed the harbor in a weird golden light while six other torpedo bearing planes swooped down for the attack.

One torpedo hit and sank the battleship Conte di Cavour. Two more damaged the battleship Littorio which was listing heavily with her bows and forecastle awash. Two Trento class cruisers were damaged, and two fleet auxiliaries had their sterns under water.

The second wave of Swordfish hit the new forty-two-thousand-ton battleship Littorio once more. It eventually settled aground. They also hit the battleship Caio Duilio which also lay with her bow aground.

Only two Swordfish were lost.

Three of the Italian battleships were out of action, one permanently and two for months to come. They withdrew most of their fleet to Naples.

The Italians lost control of the narrow Sicilian Channel and Malta lay in the center of this channel. For the British it was a crucial staging post between Gibraltar and Suez. For Germany and Italy, it was an obstruction to their supply lines.

On the other side of the world, the Japanese Navy's Commander in Chief, Admiral Isoroku Yamamoto, studied accounts of the successful British raid on ships in harbor with close interest. He even sent officers to visit Taranto. The fruits of their studies would be seen a year later at Pearl Harbor.

Malta Squadron (1940 – 1943)

The island of Malta held the central key to the control of the supply routes through the Mediterranean and along the North African coastline. Despite continual efforts by Italian and German air forces to bomb and starve the island into submission, it refused to give in. The courage and determination of its civilians and military population carried on against all odds. Among the military units on the island during those crucial times was Eight Hundred and Thirty Squadron of the Fleet Air Arm equipped with Fairey Swordfish. Its origins started in 1940 in Southern France as the Seven Hundred and Sixty Seventh Squadron of the Fleet Air Arm. They operated under the French Admiralty for raids against Italian targets.

On June 14, 1940, nine Swordfish took off from Southern France loaded with French bombs. They released twenty-three bombs on Genoa.

They were ordered to try to reach the island of Malta, a distance of 430 miles. It was just too far for them.

On June 14, two formations of twelve Swordfish left Southern France on this long flight via North African airfields to settle on the island of Malta where they joined the RAF and became Eight Hundred and Thirty Strike Force Squadron at Hal Far air station, Malta.

When the squadron arrived at Hal Far, crews were surprised to see buses all over the airfield and landed between them much to the chagrin of anti-invasion officers. The buses were put there to stop enemy aircraft landing. From this time on, the Swordfish of Eight hundred and Thirty Squadron never ceased to be a real menace and thorn in the enemy's side.

By the end of December 1940, they had sunk nine thousand tons of shipping. By November 1941, they had sunk one hundred and ten thousand tons and damaged another one hundred and thirty thousand tons of enemy shipping. Most of these ships sunk and damaged were from convoys carrying war material to the German Africa Corps in North Africa. By the end of 1942, the count had increased to four hundred thousand tons of enemy shipping, a record for one squadron never to be equaled.

This went on until 1943 with attacks on shipping, Italian harbors and airfields until only two Swordfish were left with many crew members killed or made POWs.

MAC Ships and Swordfish

MAC Ships:

Although a considerable number of Escort-Carriers were on order from American shipyards, made from pre-fabricated sections of the Liberty ships, the rate of delivery in 1943 and urgent need of them elsewhere created a problem in the central Atlantic Gap. The admiral gave the go-ahead for the conversion of grain ships and oil tankers to operate aircraft and carry cargo Merchant Aircraft Carriers or MAC ships.

They specified a minimum flight deck length of three hundred and ninety feet and the ship's speed of eleven/twelve knots, so that standard cargo hulls could be used.

The grain MAC ships had an aircraft lift and a small hangar, but tankers had no lift and no hangar but a slightly longer flight deck. The deck length was too short for takeoff of mono-planes, but the Fairy Swordfish was a biplane with considerable carrying capacity and shorter takeoff. It was an ideal weapon platform for antisubmarine operations to be flown from a MAC ship. The Swordfish was designed and built to carry a torpedo but could also carry a depth charge. Later on, the Mark III was fitted with radar and eight rockets which was considered equal to the firepower of a corvette or destroyer.

The Swordfish were pooled from Eight Hundred and Thirty Sixth, Eight Hundred and Fortieth, and Eight Hundred and Sixtieth Squadrons with a home base at RNAS Maydown in Northern Ireland. Eight Hundred and Sixtieth Squadron had three flights of eight Swordfish and were from the Royal Netherlands Navy. Ninety-two Swordfish were on duty by early 1944.

In the four months, August to November 1942, U-boats sank two hundred thousand tons of shipping, most of it in convoys. The few Escort-Carriers available were withdrawn for the North African landings. March 1943 saw ninety-seven ships sunk on the Atlantic run in twenty days. In May 1943, the first Swordfish landed aboard a MAC ship and the first MAC ships deployed with a large convoy of sixty-six merchant ships and seventeen Escorts in September 1943. It was none too soon!

By March 1944, eighteen MAC ships were operational. They ferried two hundred and twelve aircraft in eleven convoys from New York to England for the invasion of Normandy. As many as four MAC ships could be used in a convoy with sixteen Swordfish. But the usual ration was two.

Flying routine convoy protection usually meant two MAC ships worked together as a unit. Search patrols were always at the side or ahead of convoys. The last sighting of a U-boat by a Swordfish was on April 20, 1945, and the last operational flight of a Swordfish over the Atlantic was on May 1945.

MAC ships made one hundred and seventy round trips with Atlantic convoys, a total of four hundred and forty-seven days at sea. It is true to say that, since the introduction of the MAC ships into the convoy system, the U-boats had little or no success against any convoy containing them. This at a time when American troops and equipment shipped from America to Britain was at its highest.

Swordfish

The naval prototype was designated TSR, Torpedo-Spotter-Reconnaissance, and called the Swordfish. It flew for the first time on April 17, 1934. The initial production batch of eighty-six Swordfish Mark I's began delivery in February 1936. They were used on board the aircraft carriers HMS Glorious, Ark Royal, Courageous, Eagle, and Furious.

It also undertook a considerable burden of training work. After completing six hundred and ninety-two Swordfish including prototypes, the Fairey Company ceased production in 1940 to concentrate on the design, testing and manufacture of the Albacore.

Blackburn Aircraft and Motor Company built 1,699 Swordfish and continued to manufacture later versions of the Swordfish.

The last and only Swordfish in the world today is the one Fairey original saved to be a museum piece with the Fleet Air Arm Historic Flight at RNAS Yeovilton in Somerset, south of Bristol, United Kingdom.

She shall not grow old.

As we who are left to grow old.

For we will remember her.

Made in the USA
Middletown, DE
16 February 2020